DATE DUE

SE 12 97	OC 6 '06		
OC 2 97			
MY 28'98			
NO 16 98			
NO 23 '98			
NO 2 99			
BY 4 00			
AG 7 00			
SE 2 9 00			
BY 2 9 02			
NO 1 02			
BO 4 03			
DE 2 2 04			
DE 17 '05			

DEMCO 38-296

PSYCHOLOGY OF THE YOUTHFUL OFFENDER

Third Edition

PSYCHOLOGY OF THE YOUTHFUL OFFENDER

By

ROBERT N. WALKER, PH.D.

Professor of Criminal Justice, Retired
Sam Houston State University
Huntsville, Texas

CHARLES C THOMAS • PUBLISHER
Springfield • Illinois • U.S.A.

Published and Distributed Throughout the World by

CHARLES C THOMAS • PUBLISHER
2600 South First Street
Springfield, Illinois 62794-9265

© *1995 by* CHARLES C THOMAS • PUBLISHER
ISBN 0-398-06529-2   (cloth)
ISBN 0-398-06530-6   (paper)

Library of Congress Catalog Card Number: 95-16135

Second Edition, 1973
Third Edition, 1995

With THOMAS BOOKS *careful attention is given to all details of manufacturing
and design. It is the Publisher's desire to present books that are satisfactory as to their
physical qualities and artistic possibilities and appropriate for their particular use.*
THOMAS BOOKS *will be true to those laws of quality that assure a good name
and good will.*

Printed in the United States of America
SC-R-3

Library of Congress Cataloging-in-Publication Data

Walker, Robert N.
    Psychology of the youthful offender / by Robert N. Walker. — 3rd
ed.
        p.   cm.
    Includes bibliographical references and index.
    ISBN 0-398-06529-2 (cloth). — ISBN 0-398-06530-6 (paper)
    1. Juvenile delinquency—United States.   2. Juvenile delinquents—
United States—Psychology.   3. Juvenile corrections—United States.
4. Deviant behavior.   I. Title.
HV9104.W355   1995
364.3'6'019—dc20   95-16135
                                                                              CIP

Is man's civilization only a wrappage, through which the savage nature of him can still burst, infernal as ever?

... THOMAS CARLYLE

PREFACE

This textbook is the end product of over forty years of university teaching, the last ten devoted exclusively to the interaction of the criminal justice system and deviant behavior in the United States. It addresses the dismal course of society's failure to cope with today's social dilemmas.

The book is concerned with the essential social-psychological insights needed for initial safety-minimum role enactment in police, corrections and social welfare transactions involving professionals, paraprofessionals, and the public. It is also relevant to teacher education programs. It has timely relevancy.

The concise subject matter is offered as a semester-length basic text for college, pre-college and training academies. It can stand alone as a basic text in social psychology; courses in general, introductory, and/or social psychology are recommended for in-depth study of the expanding criminal justice literature now available in libraries, research centers, and publications from government auspices.

Deviant youthful behavior for years has comprised more than half of all cases compelling official cognizance by criminal justice and social welfare agencies. An understanding of the nature, motivations and criminogenic factors operating today is incumbent for all helping persons.

The pervasive harm of all types of substance abuse is obvious: narcotics, including marijuana, tobacco in all its forms, inhalants, and alcohol (the greatest abuse substance) threaten the very fabric of civilized society worldwide.

Perhaps a revolution of thinking leading to a possible decriminalization (of some drugs, especially marijuana) is indicated, as some favor. We can no longer continue mindlessly to build prisons for retribution against criminals with 50 percent or more incarcerated for drug-related offenses. Seventy-plus rates of recidivism cry for something to be done by way of a new game plan. At least a model should be tried which will view all confinement for its single valid purpose: to remove criminally inclined persons from the free world for the period of time necessary (hopefully not long) to ensure public safety and well-being.

The purpose of confinement is not "to pay a debt to society," to punish, or to exact retribution from lawbreakers (how does the convict ever "pay" for his violations by working on the rock pile for 5, 10, 20 years at a cost to taxpayers of perhaps fifty dollars per day?

Juvenile violence, ever more deadly, is closely related to easy access to guns, to the breakdown of the family (spousal abuse, teenage pregnancies, and abortions), to drug traffic which is big business in the ghetto, nullifying law enforcement efforts. Incarceration of juveniles in adult prisons without diversion which could enable some drug abuse treatment and rehabilitation must be reviewed. A less retributive system of criminal justice with the goal of eliminating the revolving-door idea is needed. Florida-type youth camps (boot camps) give regimented living a chance never experienced before and apparently have good results.

Handguns must be prohibited outside the home by adults and access to them by juveniles strictly forbidden and enforced. Handguns are clearly not needed by anyone outside the home.

AIDS is a worldwide plague of terrifying spread; society must realize its deadly nature and the need for identification of every vector (an awesome task). Intervention by public health authorities, as now used for tuberculosis and many sexually transmitted diseases using case-by-case follow-up control, would appear to be clearly needed if AIDS is ever to be checked.

Necessarily, decisions were required relative to inclusion and omission of many facets of this subject matter; the central objective of the book, to present only essential aspects, precluded inclusion of much material. This third edition is offered as a public duty by the author, who feels that a nationwide emergency rethinking is imperative relative to criminal justice's stance concerning substance abuse, juvenile violence, incarceration for retribution rather than rehabilitation, handgun control, and AIDS. Books such as this will have merit as long as social asphyxia, ignorance and misery are tolerated, as Victor Hugo declared a century and a half ago in his great novel, *Les Misérables.*

R.N.W.

CONTENTS

PSYCHOLOGY OF THE YOUTHFUL OFFENDER

Chapter 1

INTRODUCTION

The youthful offender as a recognized element of society is a social phenomenon which has developed in America during the past two decades. The rate of crimes perpetrated by youths has been steadily increasing at a rate exceeding population increases.

Statistics for crime, corrections, and public health during 1994 (the latest available at beginning of 1995) are largely accurate and meaningful only for a short time in social science. Broadbrush analyses showing trends, direction, and scope will be attempted. For example, tabulations relative to the number of children in foster homes at present will not be used.

The proportion of delinquency cases handled nonjudicially is very large. Even though it may be appropriate to handle as many cases as possible in this manner, it raises the question as to why so many that do not require judicial determination should even come to the court's attention. Police discretion at time of first arrest and nonjudicial handling of many cases, as now done, is believed to have much merit.

Juvenile delinquency cases are those referred for acts defined in the statutes of the state as the violation of a state law or municipal ordinance by children or youth of juvenile court age, or for conduct so seriously antisocial as to interfere with the rights of others or to menace the welfare of the delinquent himself, or of the community. This broad definition of delinquency includes conduct which violates the law only when committed by children, e.g., truancy, ungovernable behavior, and running away.

Method of handling cases is classified into judicial and nonjudicial, sometimes referred to as official and unofficial. "Judicial cases" are those where the court has acted on the basis of a petition or motion; "nonjudicial cases," consequently, are those cases which have been adjusted by the judge, referee, probation officer, or officer of the court without the invocation of the court's jurisdiction through petition or motion.

Why has this tremendous increase in juvenile crime come about? Who is this human being to whom we attach the label of juvenile offender?

Only by learning as much as we can about who is a juvenile offender can we answer the question of why is a juvenile offender. And only by answering the question of why is he a juvenile offender can we hope to reverse the trend toward youthful crime and perhaps channel this almost inexhaustible reservoir of power and intelligence toward constructive rather than destructive behavior.

Each individual is the unique product of his peculiar physical inheritance and the environmental shaping of that genetic endowment by social conditioning. No two individuals (other than identical twins) have the same physical endowment. Too, the environment, beginning even before conception, is unique for each individual. We are not born equal, nor do we have an equal chance to mature into productive, happy adults. We are all programmed by our ancestry, home, and school (or non-school) shaping, and many persons are in fact locked-in by shaping forces which they cannot control. This unfavorable environment operates most harmfully with the deprived and segregated residents of the so-called inner-city areas—the ghetto—who are known as the un-people: unhealthy, uneducated, unmotivated, unskilled, and unemployed.

Youths growing up in these disadvantageous settings have many built-in hurdles to overcome: poor health, overcrowded and un-hygienic housing, broken families, second-rate schools with high dropout rates, inadequate recreation, poor or non-available health services, and life-space associations which are negative or, at best, less than favorable in respect to exposure to criminal temptations. That the combination of these undesirable shaping forces results in antisocial behavior is not surprising.

Each of us is an omnibus in which our ancestors ride. If we could choose our ancestors, we might choose a little differently so that we might inherit more beauty, more intelligence, or a keener sense of humor; however, this is not for us to choose. We are blueprinted in advance by the nature and nurture of circumstances of our parents and our parents' parents. Thus, to a more or less degree, our lives are in a sense programmed. For some, the hurdles of life will prove too great to surmount; others rise above their limitations of ethnic and family milieu. We do, when we become of responsible age, enter the picture with choices that we, ourselves, make. But even then, the influences of the impressive teacher, a school counselor, a scout leader, a delinquent associate, or a neighbor can make a world of difference. The accidents of friendships or untoward contacts in our lives are highly significant, for favorable or unfavorable results. A story is often told in criminology courses about a long-legged and a short-legged boy: They both were pursued from a delinquent act—the long-legged boy outran the officers and became a priest; the short-legged boy was caught, imprisoned, and became a habitual criminal.

The social environment or milieu in which we live vitally affects our personality development and adjustment. Each of us is shaped by environmental forces, many of which are subtle and unnoticed, which operate constantly and which mold us in this direction or that. No person lives in a cultural vacuum; we are largely what our culture makes us, based on how we have reacted to these cultural forces of family, community, school, friends, work, environment, and leisure time or vacation pursuits; in short, we are what our previous experiences have made of us.

We are constantly acquiring what is largely a residual personality, an unconscious level of awareness, which shapes our conscious behavior in ways of which we are not aware. Modern learning theory holds that human conduct is largely the result of learned behavior; that the feedback from learning experiences is of critical importance in a cybernetic correction and redirection of behavior, as learned reaction patterns become fixed life-styles of behavior.

The so-called intelligence of an individual is definitely related to his chances of going to prison. The poor, unlettered, ill-dressed, unmannered, minority ethnic or racial class member is destined to comprise a disproportionate share of our prison population. It is estimated that approximately 25 percent of inmates in our prisons do not have sufficient mental ability to stay out of prison. Many are retarded, physically and/or mentally defective, illiterate or functionally illiterate (below fourth-grade levels of reading and writing), and they lack saleable job skills which could earn for them a crime-free living. They do not understand laws, are easily influenced by criminally inclined persons and cannot participate effectively in their own defense in court when under criminal trial or investigation. Such individuals are destined to be in trouble from the basic fact of their mental, emotional, and/or physical handicaps. They will continue to fill our prisons, hospitals, and relief rolls until society faces up to the need to give these handicapped and defective persons special education and job training in childhood and a sheltered environment in which they can cope throughout life. Without such training and assistance, these people will continue throughout their lives to be a costly drain on society. The question is not whether can we afford the cost of their special handling, the question is whether can we afford not to do it?

Immigrants, especially from Spanish language areas, often arrive in the United States, some with perhaps one or two years of so-called schooling. This is a serious handicap. They must start with English literacy mastery on a basic level; many lack basic understanding of a sanitary way of life, of how to use banking or money, and of laws relative to substance abuse, and motor vehicles, in order to function in daily life in a lawful society of which they had no prior experience where they lived. To counter these grave deficiencies related to the almost criminal neglect of educating children and parents in their prior environment is a serious problem in border states.

In the following chapters, we will explore the aspects of inherited tendencies, environmental shaping, and the social factors which ulti-mately result in the forming of a unique personality. We will attempt to discover why one individual becomes a well-adjusted, productive citizen and another becomes a maladjusted, youthful offender.

Our objective will be to analyze the potent social shaping forces operating during adolescence which result in adults who are, or are not, emotionally integrated, with physical and intellectual competencies which equip them to become taxpayers rather than tax burdens. We must, in fact, try to understand the adolescent animal in contemporary American society, with special reference to his special settings in the inner-city target area, which is the breeding ground for the majority of our youth-ful offenders. In this connection, the great power of the family to create or destroy its children in their adjustment to the realities of life will be given primary recognition: The child forecasts the man as the dawn forecasts the day, and behind each disturbed child one can often find a maladjusted parent or parent surrogate (e.g., guardian, uncle).

This text is specifically intended to provide a brief and concise cover-age available to assist police, corrections, and social rehabilitation stu-dents and practitioners in their increasingly frequent adversary or helping encounters with youthful offenders. The pitch of this book is that of the medical model: not to confront the client, or patient, child, or respon-dent with recriminations and blame; rather, to proceed in a therapeutic manner to salvage what can be saved from the threatened wreck of youthful lives as social agencies impact with the turbulence and immatu-rity of the adolescent years. In short, to help the officer, probationer and others involved with the manner society deals with the youth, and to search for causes and possible cures instead of the details of specific acts with a view to punitive action to follow, is the goal of this book.

To punish is to harm, especially with children of tender years (perhaps age 14 or lower). Confinement is rarely, if ever, a therapeutic environment. We are seeking to reverse a life of failure under difficult conditions, and success usually does not follow. Recidivism runs about 70 percent. Yet violent criminal behavior must be controlled. Safety of the public is the first duty of government. Regrettably, some individuals (many mentally ill) must be confined today for a period of time, hopefully not long. Some chronically ill mental patients (not to be regarded as convicts) may require years of closed-ward control in a hospital setting.

Chapter 2

PSYCHOLOGY AND PHYSIOLOGY

Every police or corrections officer (including nurses, teachers, counselors) is a practicing psychologist, and every interpersonal encounter—whether an adversary confrontation or a helping act—demands insights which the science of psychology today can provide. Without these essential safety-minimum understandings, professional conduct and even lives are jeopardized. This book's purpose is to identify and explain these basic behavioral concepts in order to minimize malpractices and, hopefully, to contribute to a higher level of professional functioning by all who must interact with the public in police, corrections, or social role enactments.

No valid estimates can be made relative to the proportion of the criminal or non-criminal population who at any time are mildly or severely mentally ill. It is believed that millions of individuals are at large in this country who are either temporarily or permanently out of touch with reality; for them the real world is a cloudy, indistinct, and transient state of conscious awareness. Added to this number are those countless thousands who by use of mind-altering substances (alcohol notably, and drugs) envelope themselves in a chemical cocoon and depart from the real world for limited periods of time.

A condition of mild emotional maladjustment which each of us commonly exhibits during stress—often called a psychoneurosis—is differentiated from psychosis by the ability of the neurotic individual to maintain insight, that is, an awareness that some fears, compulsions, and inappropriate behaviors are present in his behavior but departure from the real world is at times shown. The individual functions in the present and retains contact with persons and places, although at times on less-than-optimum levels of efficiency or comfort. More definitive explanations of mental illness will be given in the following pages.

The word psychology is derived from two Greek words: *psyche* (mind, emotions, feelings, thinking, reason, the mental life, impulsive activities and predispositions) and *ology* (study of). Psychology seeks to comprehend, to predict and to control behavior.

In this text our focus is on deviant social behavior of a nature compelling either formal or informal attention from the criminal justice system or school authorities in order for interdependent social life to exist.

This is not a textbook on the treatment of mental illness; it is concerned with psychotherapy only to sensitize police and corrections officers in order that mental illness will not be aggravated by preventable malpractices. It will seek to identify, diagnose, and explore the essential causal factors which result in the human dilemma of crime, violence, ignorance, and misery—a predicament which threatens the very existence of today's society.

This text will treat briefly the minimum essentials of behavior theory, believed to be necessary for professional role enactment by today's police or corrections officer. In the interest of brevity, much material which would be valuable for elaboration of concepts has been omitted. Selection of content has been arbitrarily done by the author, based on this lifetime of teaching psychology and his recent decade of teaching precisely this subject matter to thousands of pre- and in-service officers; the benefit of their cybernetic feedback of suggestions and experience in this connection is gratefully acknowledged.

Officers are practicing psychologists, whether they realize it or not, and interact every day, every hour, with the entire spectrum of helping persons. Both criminal and non-criminal (civil) behaviors are by social directive the responsibility of official helping agencies. The professional officer cannot function today without essential insights into the scientific nature of human behavior. No longer may "odd" behavior be glibly explained away by yesterday's myths relative to inherited moral depravity or predestined determinism or environmental distortions of reality. Instead, a dispassionate consideration of the developmental causes of mental illness (and criminal manifestations of it) and their physical and environmental aspects is essential.

All officers must be able to recognize the presence of mental illness in an officer-citizen encounter (an adversary confrontation or a social assistance act). Finally, the appropriate action which is professionally indicated will hopefully be considered. Obviously no cookbook recipe is usable in incidents involving "odd behavior." Nor is it the expectation of this introductory course that competent practitioners of mental hygiene can be created. Rather, it is hoped that essential insights will have been gained in order to minimize malpractices; to reduce harm to ill persons; to salvage as much as possible from dangerous and damaged cases; and hopefully to improve the mental hygiene of the individual officer student as a person, as a family man, and as a public servant. Some eighty percent of your work is social welfare in nature; this text is directly focused on such aspects.

A review of basic psychology and some reference to anthropology and genetics, useful as a prelude to the main body of the text, follows:

Man in relatively his present form has been on earth for at least some 1.75 million years, according to the National Geographic Society. He has been relatively civilized only for the past 10,000 years. A little alcohol, drugs, fever, anger, or mental illness and his behavior reverts to savagery. The thin veneer of civilization is man's predicament.

Doctor Sigmund Freud (1856–1939) said of himself (Freud, undated) that he was not a great man but that he had made a great discovery: the world of the unconscious (psychological processes taking place at the hidden levels of the personality), in which has been recorded all that has ever happened to us and which shapes our conscious behavior in ways of which we are not aware. Professor Sarason (1994) has credited Freud with a great contribution to psychology.

The human brain is in many respects like a data processing machine: it receives, classifies, stores, and retrieves information (input) from sensory receptors; this memory bank (stream of conscious) is what we use to cope with life's adjustment requirements and as feedback correction for new learnings and behavior.

The human brain, an organ of the body, is subject to the same physical laws as other organs. The remarkable thing is that it functions most of the time as well as it does. Organic conditions which are positively related to mental illness are:

Genetic defects (of inheritance) or birth injury
Brain defect tumor (cancerous) or from aging (senility)
Arteriosclerosis (hardening of the arteries with deficient oxygen supply to brain tissues—related to clouded sensorium)
Diseases of the brain (syphilis, meningitis, Alzheimer's)
Trauma to the brain (blows, falls)
Toxic substances (chronic alcoholism, narcotic intoxication, lead poisoning, chemical inhalants)
Nutritional deficiencies, endocrine system dysfunction and imbal-

ance in brain chemistry. Recently, vitamin supplements have shown promise in cases of Down's syndrome.

Drug abuse (all kinds, including alcohol, marijuana, and tobacco)

Interrupted airway to lungs (asphyxia from crushes, drowning, glue sniffing)

CVA—cerebral vascular accidents (stroke)

Another category of mental illness, called functional, because the sick person is unable to function efficiently, has no demonstrable physical evidence of organic defect. However, the patient can be as sick as with an organic condition; often, both conditions occur concurrently,

Each of us has a psyche (mind, reason, emotions) and a soma (body) which are in reciprocal relationship to each other; that is, the one affects the other. Ill health of the emotions affects the body and vice versa. We can and do think ourselves into sickness or health. Some 75 to 95 percent of physical illness is believed by medical authorities to originate in the emotions. Even the common cold is considered to be related to emotional well-being. Gastric ulcers, dermatitis, asthma, and migraine headaches are clearly related to emotional stress.

Mental illness cases occupy half of all hospital beds, and one person in every ten will probably spend some time in some controlled environment. Widespread recent use of tranquilizing medications has enabled perhaps half of those who would have been hospital patients to be treated as outpatients and to remain at work and at home, with great savings in hospital costs. Long-term effects of these drugs, possibly deleterious, are not now known, but toxic side effects are possible from prolonged self-medication.

Mental illness today is recognized as a legitimate form of illness and the stigma from this category of illness is not what it used to be. However, for many people, the "mysterious" nature of mental illness and its understanding and rational acceptance by the general public is still far from universal. All stigma should be removed from mental illness; the general public holds distorted views and much enlightenment is needed in this matter.

The simple fact is that each of us is never "normal" all the time, and we each have mental hygiene conditions ranging from some "shade of gray," from very dark and sick to very light and relatively adjusted emotional states. Every person can be brought to a condition of "breakdown" (emotional collapse) if the stress is severe enough and applied long enough; there is no superhuman person who can cope forever with overwhelming stress.

The history of care for mentally ill persons is a deplorable account of inhumane neglect and cruelty. Even today, conditions in some closed-ward hospitals are shocking, with therapy almost completely neglected; "warehouse" confinement is its best description. Today's mental hygiene movement attempts to foster humane care and preventive measures for mental illness. Open-ward, family care, and outpatient consultation services are available in many—but unfortunately not all—places. Mental illness must be treated promptly before the patient gets secondary gain from his symptoms in the form of sympathy, excuse from work, or financial reward.

Myth in medicine, which physicians fortunately can use, is powerful medicine: this is the patient's belief that the physician has power to help illness; confidence in one's physician is a valuable help to recovery.

There are many evidences of psychodynamic motivations to human behavior; the following are clear examples:

> Compulsive theft (girl stealing a sweater, then discarding it outside the store)
> Bed-wetting, negative behavior to get even with a parent
> Psychosomatic illness: the mind causes the body to be sick (headaches)
> Freudian slips of the tongue; accidents which appear to be wished for (fingers in a lawn mower)
> Battered child syndrome (displaced aggression; child murders by mothers)
> Malingering (nesting) patient who unconsciously resists efforts to cure him, and wishes to remain in bed or in hospital for secondary gain
> Sexual acting-out behavior (promiscuity for girl; fathering a baby by boy)

Adjustment mechanisms (to cope with stress) are recognized:

> Illness (most used)
> Fantasy
> Sublimation
> Repression
> Projection
> Identification
> Substitution

Regression
Compensation
Conversion reaction (emotional stress into physical condition)

These mechanisms have unconscious bases and invite therapy. Compulsive theft is an example of unconscious dynamic motivations based on hostility and aggression, with perhaps elements related to seeking of self-punishment (macochism); desire to sexual thrill; seeking to hurt parents, spouse, and family; ventilating of hostility; and surfacing of compulsions to hurt, destroy, and vandalize.

This brief survey of abnormal psychology is in no sense complete. Students are encouraged to learn more in structured courses on the college or university levels. Mental illness is unfortunately often observed in the inner-city and competitive stress in life-styles for minority persons. Daily life is almost social asphyxia for many there. It must be realized that there is no color bar to mental illness and that it crosses all lines of race, income, residence, education, and social classes.

Persons in helping relations must be able to recognize cases of both mild and severe mental illness and then should refer such cases for definitive professional help. Mental illness, either mild, situational or long-term severe, is illness and the need for therapy urgently exists. These cases do not get well spontaneously, and if neglected progress to critical life-threatening levels, with great cost to society.

Bed-wetting is believed not to be under the child's conscious control before about age three. Many children are punished for it by caregivers who are ignorant of this medical fact (sphincter control related to age).

There is no known proportion as to whether behavior is shaped, say, 80 percent by the environment and 20 percent from inherited factors, or the opposite, of half and half. Both heredity and environment operate with each of us and all the time. We are omnibuses in which our ancestors ride. Defects related to birth, accidents, injuries (trauma), aging, and toxic substances are clearly of organic nature. A constitutional (physical body) inferiority is unfortunately the inheritance of some individuals; their prognosis for adjustment to life is poor; some do achieve remarkable success with medication and intensive therapy.

The social environment or milieu in which we live vitally affects our personality development and adjustment. Each of us is shaped by environmental forces, many of which are subtle and unnoticed, which operate constantly and which mold us in this direction or that. No person lives in a cultural vacuum; we are largely what our culture makes us, based on how we have reacted to these cultural forces of family, community, school, friends, work environment, and leisure time or vacation pursuits; in short, we are what our previous experiences have made us.

We are constantly acquiring what is largely a residual personality, an unconscious level of awareness, which shapes our conscious behavior in ways of which we are not aware. Modern learning theory holds that human conduct is largely the result of learned behavior; that the feedback from learning experience is of crucial importance in a cybernetic correction and redirection of behavior, as learned reaction patterns become fixed life-styles of behavior. It is believed that experiences of living are indelibly remembered and shape both conscious and unconscious behavior in ways not realized on a conscious level.

The so-called "intelligence" (i.e., mental maturity in ratio to chronological age) of an individual is definitely related to criminal behavior and his chances of going to prison. The poor, unlettered, ill-dressed, unmannered, minority ethnic or racial class member is destined to comprise a disproportionate share of our prison population until society ceases to be part of the problem by its neglect of children, defective education, discrimination, and racism.

Modern endocrine research has enabled many individuals who would have been destined to lead defective lives to function normally. Advances in medical knowledge which the future will bring may revolutionize today's concept of the relation of glandular function and DNA to human behavior.

Nutritional and vitamin deficiencies are directly related to some mental illness. Prisoner-of-war camps have long shown what deprivation of proper diet can cause by way of psychotic reactions; even the will to live can be extinguished. Brain damage from trauma, toxic substance, infection, tumors, and aging are obviously of organic nature. Prolonged alcoholic and drug intoxication escalates to brain damage with irreversible changes in brain tissue and psychotic behavior. Lead poisoning is an example of toxic-induced mental disturbance; it still is found in ghetto children who ingest lead paint. Glue and cleaning fluid sniffing for purposes of "a high" is extremely dangerous; fatal or irreversible damage may be caused by oxygen blockage from asphyxia, as well as kidney and liver failure.

Degenerative changes resulting from aging are important causes of mental illness. Since our population is increasingly composed of older persons, this category of mental illness can be expected to concern us more as time passes. Public agency interaction with aged persons will increase as their absolute and relative numbers increase. Modern medicine has prolonged lives of many older persons with consequent multiplication of problems in caring for them. When the brain does not receive oxygen because of arteriosclerosis (hardening of the arteries) commonly found in later life, or trauma, there may be a resulting decrease in efficiency of living: forgetfulness, confusion, poor judgment, distortion of reality, and clouded sensorium. A gross anatomical deterioration of brain tissue is shown with advanced age (Alzheimer's cases).

The brain is subject to all of the defects of the rest of our organic system and in addition develops its own illness syndromes and defects. The consequences of a brief loss of oxygen for just a minute or two (3 to 5 minutes at the most) may cause permanent irreparable damage.

The consequences of genetic defects (birth anomalies), drug addiction of newborn, too much or too little oxygen at birth, possibilities of trauma, blows, concussion, disease, foreign objects, and toxins related to the brain area—all can cause brain damage and/or defects.

The following physical conditions, among others, affect the brain:

DISEASES AND DEFECTS

> Spinal meningitis
> Chronic alcoholism ("pickles" the brain)
> Brain syndromes
> Fever
> Syphilis
> Hemorrhages, embolisms, little strokes (cerebrovascular accident) related to arteriosclerosis (hardening of the arteries)
> Convulsive disorders
> Encephalitis
> Meningitis
> Measles
> HIV/AIDS

CONSEQUENCES OF DRUG ABUSE

> Mind-expanding drugs (flashbacks, chromosome changes)
> Addiction from entire spectrum of psychedelic pharmaceuticals
> Chronic obstructive pulmonary diseases from cigarette smoking or secondary smoke inhalation

CHEMICALS

Lead (brings toxic condition, with convulsions)
Gases
Glues, aerosols, solvents (many bring about permanent irreversible damage from even short period deprivation of oxygen to brain).

DEGENERATIVE DISEASES

Brain atrophy (brain undergoes gross anatomical deterioration related to aging)

TRAUMA

Accidents, occupational and vehicle injuries, and athletics—for example, boxing is no longer a major intercollegiate sport.

Mental illness (mild or severe, temporary or long-lasting) is defined herein as a definite state of mental disequilibrium in which inappropriate and inefficient behavior is acted out and which may or may not be criminal in nature. The cause may be organic or functional or a combination of the two. Functional mental illness is evidenced by inability to operate effectively in daily living and for which organic causal factors remain unidentified.

PERSONALITY THEORIES

Personality is defined as an individual's dynamic behavior system stemming from his conscious and unconscious life-space perceptions. Allport's definition is perhaps the best known: "Personality is the dynamic organization within the individual of those psychophysical systems that determine his characteristic behavior and thought. . . . Personality is something and does something . . . it is what lies behind specific acts and within the individual" (Allport, 1960).

Personality is rough hewn by heredity and shaped and refined by the environment. The yearly years are of the greatest importance since the personality is most plastic and malleable at that time; later reshaping of the personality is always possible, but at great cost of time and effort. The human personality appears to be melted and reshaped anew during the adolescent period.

There are a number of personality theories which attempt to explain human behavior: behaviorism (John B. Watson), connectionism (E. L.

Thorndike), classical conditioning (I. P. Pavlov), operant conditioning (B. F. Skinner), psychoanalytic (Sigmund Freud), Neo-Freudian (Karen Horney), self-theory (Carl Rogers), and existential psychology (Heidegger). The Neo-Freudians insist upon the relevance of social psychological variables against the strong instinctive views of the Freudians.

Each of these theoretical positions has merit and deserves consideration at the reader's leisure; we will briefly survey herein the views of Doctors Freud and Skinner.

The role of conscious memory as shaper of conscious behavior is undoubtedly important. Dream life, free reverie, hypnotic behavior, accidents of living, slips of the tongue, doodling, electric stimulation of brain areas, sleepwalking, forgetfulness (e.g., dental appointments), multiple personality, parapraxes, and sudden insightful solutions to problems, all have relationship to unconscious mental processes.

Sigmund Freud, M.D. (1856–1939) said of himself that he did not believe he was a great man, but he did believe that he had made a great discovery: the world of the unconscious. He postulated that all impressions (learnings and experiences) which we gain from living are recorded in our memory and cannot be cancelled out. All is received, classified, stored, and retrieved by the twelve billion or so cells of the brain. We are shaped from earliest infancy by the process of living. This subtle and insidious process goes on without our being aware of its operation. The feedback from experience of living, with some behavior rewarded and strengthened and some punished and inhibited, is what molds and conditions our personality. Doctor Freud believed in the significance of mental factors in the different vital functions as well as in illnesses and their treatment, and that sex played a great part in personality shaping, with fixations on parental figures (the father for girls, the mother for boys) which he called the Oedipal relationship or family romance.

Since sexual outlets are controlled by customs and laws, a great deal of frustration and conflict accompanies it. Trauma (shocks) from sexual experiences in early life are often related to later emotional maladjustments and even to serious mental illness, in Freud's view. Psychodynamic processes involving the unconscious are involved in creative thinking, artistic production, and religious experience.

Freud said there were three levels of personality: id (primitive urges), ego (reality principle), and superego (conscience). He believed the task of the psychotherapist was to bring to the conscious level that which is unconscious and that mental illness could be treated by deep analysis of the unconscious levels of personality. He said there was both a life instinct and a death instinct which operates in all persons. He developed theories of dream analysis with both latent (hidden) and manifest (apparent) aspects, and interpreted the symbols found in dreams; dreams were indications of wish-fulfillment of deep unconscious needs.

Hypnosis as a therapeutic tool was abandoned by Freud because the patient does not remember what happens during hypnotic sleep. Freud wanted the patient to help with his own treatment, which is a requirement in all psychotherapy.

For Freud, conflict and frustration are the name of the game for humans, and this means that some mental illness for some people is to be regarded as an inevitable consequence of living. We have physical, psychological, and cultural barriers which thwart expressions of personality. When these blocks are not resolved or are not effectively adjusted to, hostility, aggression, sexual difficulties, and both psychological and physiological stress inevitably results. Every individual has a breaking point which cannot be passed without physical or emotional damage. The end process is a psychological casualty functioning inefficiently in life's struggle, or even in the closed ward of a mental hospital.

Doctor Freud formulated theories relative to the oral, anal, phallic, latent, and genital periods of human sexual development and their psychological implications. You are invited to read his perceptive writings.

Aggression has been given much importance by Freud, as expressed directly, by physical or verbal assaults, or indirectly (vicariously) as in watching boxing. Hostility toward authority, compulsive theft, suicide, battered child syndrome, sexual assaults, murder, contact sports, hunting, spectator sports such as bullfighting, punching a bag, are all related to deep personality traits and reflect destructive forces of instinctive nature. Their dynamic power to shape human behavior is evident.

Anxiety is defined as a psychophysical reaction to threat; it is a sign of danger which the individual then uses to initiate adjustment countermeasures to restore equilibrium. Some anxiety is free-floating without reference to a specific cause. Anxiety is both a cause of physical stress and can result from it, with inescapable somatic involvement of glandular, muscular, and visceral organs. The executive's gastric ulcer is an example of a psychogenic illness.

Birth trauma is the first anxiety-provoking threat experienced by the individual. Anxiety is a symptom used by mentally ill persons and has utility for them. They get secondary gain from their symptom and the symptom serves a purpose: to gain attention, sympathy, excuse from work, and to mask to real basic underlying stress factor causing the symptom. Treating the symptom and removing it will not cure the basic causal factor. The symptom may be a useful defense which the patient employs unconsciously to excuse or to rationalize out of his present impasse situation. Anxiety is the basic symptom for all emotional disorders.

Guilt and anxiety are related, and the dynamic consequences of both are stress reactions involving both physical and psychological aspects of behavior. Condition red which is a generalized physiological response to fear, rage, or love, involves the entire body (soma). The polygraph's operation with the autonomic nervous system's independent working exemplifies this physical response. The psychological response to severe and chronic anxiety is depression and disintegration of personality, with both emotional and physical evidences (e.g., depression, insomnia, indigestion).

Trauma in the form of death, temporary separations, hospitalizations, weaning, entering school, marriage, and family terminal disintegration are anxiety-provoking for all persons.

Guilt, in the form of self-blame, is inevitable for all of us. We fail both by omission and commission as we pass along life's trials from birth to death. Guilt involves fantasy and introspection, with remorse, regrets, and self-incrimination, often with no useful purpose to be served. The role of confession as a safety valve for guilt is recognized. Suicide has a guilt aspect which is overladen with hostility, even to the point of self-destruction.

Freud's original thinking and restatement of other thinking in a new context is shown in the theoretical and technical innovations which flowed from such concepts as the following:

> The Dynamic Unconscious
> Transference
> Narcissism
> Resistance
> Rationalization
> Symptom Formation—The symptoms of illness can be shown to serve the unconscious needs of the patient.
> The Neurotic Conflict
> Fixation
> Conversion

Displacement
Object Relationships—Cathexis
Dream Analysis—The dreamer often expresses in his dreams wishes
   of which he is unaware, on a level of full awareness.
Libido
Freudian Slips of the Tongue (Parapraxes)
Life and Death Instincts
Pleasure Principle—Immediate Gratification
Reality Principle—Deferred gratification
Repression—Need to "ventilate" the unconscious

You are invited to read Freud's works or any standard text in abnormal psychology for elaboration of the above.

Id—biological, primary, primitive, elemental animal impulses; reservoir of instinctual urges, basic, unrefined, and unbridled drives, such as lust and aggression, a seething cauldron of vicious hedonistic passions hidden deep within the core of personality, id operates on the pleasure principle and is present at birth. It interacts with ego and superego, if and when it can circumvent them. The id is the repository of selfish instincts, but if there were no taboos there would be no gratifications; hence, we now have some gratification for all, but not all for some.

Ego—the reality principle, the executive and social component of the personality; it perceives, thinks, feels, and does, and takes a stand against the pleasure seeking of the id. Parents use guilt and punishment to control children; this is reality.

Superego—the conscience; the internalization of all the external controls that play upon the individual. It is grown at home, from earliest conditioning by feedback from intrafamily interaction: The mother's role is crucial. Some individuals are lacking in all superego controls; they are the product of a loveless rearing.

The mind can be likened to an iceberg; the smaller part above the surface is the region of consciousness, the much larger mass below water is the region of the unconscious: urges, passions, the repressed ideas and feelings, the great underworld of vital, unseen forces which exercise an imperious control over the conscious thoughts and acts of man.

Freud's theory is one explanation, among others, in studying the behavior of man. He was such an intellectual giant that all who follow him in a sense ape him and must use much of his terminology. Freud's theory tries to envisage man as an animal beset with instinctual drives, living in a hostile world, with reason not a basis for life; man is in the predicament of knowing, as no other animal does, that he must die. Freud postulated that the etiology of mental illness must be discovered in order to achieve its therapy (abreaction, catharsis).

This text has been written with a strong debt to Doctor Freud and his great contributions to understanding human behavior. Freud was undoubtedly a pioneer thinker in his encyclopedic survey of human behavior of his times and with much insight useful for today. He has received criticism from the psychology profession for his unscientific (that is, his cases resist replication and modern application) writings, but his place seems secure among the truly great minds of the past century.

Professor Sarason (1994, pp. 13–15) credits Freud with the following important psychological insights:

1. Directed attention to infantile and childhood sexuality.

2. He made the world aware of how complicated, nuanced, and multimotivated impersonal and family relationships are . . . that irrationality and destructive aggression are part and parcel of human heritage.

3. Nature and function of dreams—not random, did not have simple explanations. (Dreams in criminal court case—O. J. Simpson's case.)

4. The irrational in human beings—inevitable, untamable, and frequently explosively destructive.

At the other swing of the pendulum of behavior theory, and with diametric opposite position, is Dr. B. F. Skinner, perhaps the most influential American psychologist of recent times. Known as operant (instrumental) reinforcement theory, its central idea is that when behavior which is wanted appears, it is to be reinforced with immediate reward. The animal (human or infra-human) does something and gets something. In contrast to Pavlovian classical conditioning, where the dog either salivated or did not, the experimental subject in the Skinner Box is active and has a choice of several possible behaviors. The specific behavior which is desired is paid off promptly when it is manifested. Skinner believes man's life is now programmed by external controls, and the best good for all will be a world where social controls will be designed to reward behavior which is good for society: freedom, as now experienced in the Western world, will be lost to a pattern of life like the discipline of Red China. Behavior is shaped and maintained by its consequences, he maintains. A strict behavioristic psychologist, he accords no place to depth factor of personality, instincts, or inner life of cognitive processes. Environments are defective when they fail to make desirable behavior pay off or when they resort primarily to revengeful punishment as a means of deterring or stopping undesirable behavior.

Mental hospitals, schools, governments (China and Russia notably) have used Skinnerian reinforcement to shape behavior in directions desired, with effective results. Operant conditioning brings many forms of behavior under stimulus control, for deliberate manipulation toward a desired goal. The possibility exists that human society may indeed be transformed by widespread application of this social theory.

Chapter 3

THE FAMILY

The tremendous influence of the home and family in shaping every child toward a satisfactory life adjustment or a collision course with disaster cannot be overestimated. The family constellation is a most potent and subtle shaping force, with much of its effects not realized on a conscious level of recall. Here is where personality in its most plastic and malleable form becomes jelled, concretized and structured. It is only with great difficulty that the personality as shaped in early years (to age 4) can be remolded in later life.

The child is developing his personality from his very first breath, and the sooner the shaping forces of conformity and the development of a superego (a conscience) is performed, the better.

The human personality is today believed to be shaped by forces which may be either within or without the psyche—that is, human behavior is the result of learnings which are the feedback of experience as these experiences build on the genetic endowment through living. Whether one interprets the theoretical basis of behavior in terms of behaviorism (Drs. Watson and Skinner, 1972), psychoanalytic theory (Dr. Freud) (Gay, 1988), learning theory, or some eclectic mixture of these extremes, the fact remains that human behavior is the result of both heredity and environment as shaped by social conditioning.

Differential exposure to environmental forces is of great importance, but the genetic endowment also cannot be overlooked. It is believed today that no person is born to be anything; he has a potential, which may or may not be maximally realized as his environment and his peculiar reaction to that environment determine the final product. We are, in fact, born grossly unequal; to a considerable extent our lives are programmed by our ancestry, our parental socioeconomic and racial circumstances, and our neighborhood, schools, and non-school environment. Some accidental incidents may cause profound consequences. This is not to say that anyone is destined to his place in life. Each of us is

23

today what our yesterdays made us, and we will be tomorrow what our todays are making us. We grow our personalities by living them.

Each individual is believed to require the experience of T.L.C. (tender, loving care) for his full emotional development. The superego, or conscience, must be learned. Empathy, compassion, and social responsibility seem to be conspicuously lacking in many adolescents today who are turned off from society. These seemingly cold and detached young people are believed often to have grown up where these qualities were not present in their structuring environment. The home is clearly implicated as creator of his condition. We act as we do because of feedback from our experiences, from the fallout. The technical term for this process is cybernetics. Some parents have apparently abdicated from their traditional role enactment. Children are tolerated at home as they show incorrigibility, disobedience to reasonable intra-family controls, and even drug abuse. Today one often observes an absence of parental authority, the pater familias concept, which has been a salient aspect in German, Italian, Greek, and Chinese immigrant first-generation families during the past century in America. This breakdown of parental authority and responsibility is deplored by many sociologists; its pernicious effects are evident: physical and verbal assaults on teachers and police, as well as sometimes serious parental discontrol.

The family is of the utmost importance in the social conditioning process. It is the twig-bender whose subtle and covert effects cannot be overemphasized. The small child is, from birth, responding either favorably or unfavorably either toward or away from social adjustment, to all the input of learning from his living. These learnings have feedback corrective effects on his behavior. He will tend to repeat that behavior which is painful and/or unrewarding, as Professor E. L. Thorndike taught early in this century in his theory of connectionism. Doctor Skinner's operant conditioning theory, with prompt rewarding for behavior which is desired by the experimenter, appears to have great potential as a device to shape mass behavior, as evidenced in North Korea and China today and for decades past where deliberate and designed environmental conditioning is being applied to millions of humans with the announced purpose of creating a new Socialist Man. No input of ideas is tolerated which could possibly dilute or weaken the thinking of their citizens in exactly the direction desired. Every effort is made by all media and laws at the government's disposal to disparage and falsify any thinking which may be subversive or revisionist. Conformity in thinking and acting is mandatory as desired by governmental authorities.

The family shapes in insidious ways, and we are not aware of the shaping which goes on very subtly, in homeopathic doses, minute portions. The family is where our attitudes are laid down. It is where we get our religious orientation and our political convictions, where we develop our ideas of racism, of intolerance or of tolerance, of respect or hatred for others. It is a closed environment, at a time when the child is most plastic and receptive. He has no frame of reference to combat the ideas which are repetitively implanted day after day—not only by precept but much more effectively by examples. For example, some parents teach their children to kill themselves on the road by the way the parent drives: no regard for traffic laws, speeding, and reckless disregard of road courtesy. The child sees this and repeats it when he/she is the driver.

The parents' way of life rubs off—whether the family pays its bills or is a family of deadbeats, whether they are self-sufficient or predators on the neighbors, whether the grass is cut and debris cleared away or a slum created at home.

By the time a child enters school, he is very thoroughly indoctrinated and shaped. Even four years of college changes attitudes very little in respect to racial tolerance, political bigotry, or religious orientation. Education does not necessarily erase misconceptions that are grossly untenable.

The family's closed environment during the most formative years gives the opportunity to build both conscious and unconscious value systems, a philosophy of life and style of life which is of marked permanence throughout life. The fallout from living in intimate daily interaction with parents (and here the mother's role is crucial), and significant others in the family circle, leaves permanent deep personality shaping which often may result in pathological behavior in later life. Perceptions of reality (we see things not as they are but as we are) are clearly related to prior learnings from living.

This poses a dilemma. The family shapes us, but many times in ways that are not wholesome. Surveys indicate that while the majority of today's parents are high school graduates, we have millions of Americans who are illiterate. Statistics also indicate that, generally speaking, parents who are uneducated have more children than do those who have attained a higher level of formal education. At one time in our history, a large family was thought to be the best family. Social attitudes now, however, tend to place more value on quality than on quantity. The resources of every family must be divided among the members of that family. And too often economic necessity still is one of the forces resulting in early school dropout for the children of a large family with lower income.

That many homes are patently intolerable and unwholesome is indicated by statistics which estimate that more than a million children ran away from home last year in the United States. The mother's role in the family cannot be underscored too strongly. She is the key person. Biographies of the great achievers in our society (Lincoln among them) indicate the great debt they owe to their mothers. The mother who works at the job of being a mother, offering the encouragement, the security, the smiling serenity that is priceless, has a God-given role, and the result of how effectively that role is fulfilled is largely in her hands with great consequences for society. Being a good mother, however, does not mean being an indulgent mother. It is cruelty to be overindulgent with children. Indulgence too often is an expression not of love but of taking the easy way out. Discipline is a basic requirement for the healthy maturation of a child's character. So-called smother-love, where the mother gets her emotional needs from the child (usually an only child), and where the husband is almost a nonentity, is a great threat to the child's healthy emotional maturation.

✳The mother who rejects her child, either consciously or unconsciously, does irreparable damage to the child. Frequently, a mother rejects her child because she feels he will spoil her career by keeping her from work or because he hampers her freedom for social activities or simply because she is not mature enough herself to accept the responsibility of a child. She says that she loves the child dearly, but her actions, her body language, tell a different story. And the child senses this rejection. Even a newborn baby senses the lack of warmth, the support, the bodily fondling and caressing. Such children are often retarded in growth and show emotional difficulties very early in life, with unfavorable prognosis for good adjustment later in life.

If a mother does not really cherish her child, the child senses it. Orphanage children may show extreme emotional difficulties later in life because of the deprivation resulting from early life impersonal environment. The mother's role is to see to it that the child's physical and emotional needs are anticipated and met and that the child feels secure; the institutional environment of an orphanage rarely can provide that emotional security. However, it is possible that quality institutional care in some cases may be superior to the gross neglect often observed in ghetto areas. The orphanages of Dickens' day are not models for today, where children lack shelter, adult care, meals and medical attention. These cases call for professional intervention, especially where the caregiver is deficient in resources and knowledge. If the private sector is not doing the job, social services must help. Children must be cared for. Experiments in a few more progressive institutions with substitute mothers have been highly successful. These women, mostly volunteers, come in to the institution on a regular basis and do nothing but love and cuddle the babies, rock them, play with them, and give them the emotional warmth which the regular staff often cannot find time to do.

Child-rearing practices show marked differences from culture to culture and are believed, in Freudian theory, to have direct relationship in many cases to adult mental illness. Weaning, breast feeding, rigid toilet training, neglect, rejection, infrequent mothering, smother-love, corporal punishment (the battered child syndrome), the whole pattern of child care practices are of the greatest importance in personality shaping. Those children who lack the three L's (Love, Limitations, and Let Them Grow Up) (Sahakian, 1968) are likely to develop distortions of reality and possibly neurotic or even psychotic tendencies or conditions in later life. The role of the mother or the parent surrogate is crucial in the shaping of the styles of life which will be the later personality pattern of each child. The responding significant adult interaction with the child can build security or insecurity; absence of love, confidence, and support is believed to be extremely deleterious for wholesome personality development. This view is today given great validity by authorities in psychopathology.

Many of the ways of life and child-rearing practices commonly associated with black families are, in fact, more properly descriptions of lower socioeconomic classes, white, black, or brown. There are high rates of broken homes (especially early desertion from family responsibilities by the father); non-concern for future contingencies of life; shifting of family care responsibilities to older siblings, grandparents, or social agencies; and minimal attention to whether the essentials of family life are adequately provided—shelter, food, economic support and emotional security. Where the family unit is a matriarchy, the boy is denied an exemplar to follow toward achieving a masculine role identity into manhood. Some individuals, like Ralph Bunch, succeed against the odds.

Parental shaping—the language used, their ways of relating, the taboos which they unconsciously hold, their value systems, and role enactments and expectations—is extremely formative with children who are in the most malleable and receptive period of their lives. These subtle influences which are all-pervasive are by social osmosis absorbed into the very fabric of the lives of children, without conscious awareness. We teach much more by example than by precept, and these examples transcend ethnic, religious, or social class origins.

Interaction within the family constellation is also to be considered; reciprocally interrelating roles must be defined, with the potential ever present for distortions of reality which can be pathogenic. In the family, the basic social roles are learned, social values are defined, and the forecast for much of life's subsequent path is shaped. Infants are in fact acculturated and acclimatized, with the process largely completed by age three. Doctor Freud has always held to his theory of the enduring and often ineradicable effect of fallout from early childhood. Shaping in the family has been most fundamental to this theory of personality development and its psychopathology.

Also basic in Freudian theory is the view that early life experiences within the family constellation cannot be fully reshaped or undone. Children with severe emotional disturbances are almost without exception the product of being raised in a very faulty family setting. A child's cognitive development is initiated within the family circle. Children with organic mental illness from disease or injury require special therapy.

Deprivation of rich sensory input (including emotional security) during early months of life is today believed likely to jeopardize later realization of possible intellectual potential. The first eighteen months to thirty-six months of life are seen as crucial periods, when the quality of every child's mental, emotional, and physical composition is largely being firmly defined, with great possibilities for less than optimum realization being related to what occurs in the home during that time.

How the mother's role as provider of nourishment, care, and love is performed or neglected is known to affect the intelligence, health, and maturation of all the various ages of the child—emotional, mental, social, and even psychological. The richness or poverty of stimulating experiences in the first few months of life are of extreme importance to optimum development. Rejection by the mother of a child's basic need for security and affection is promptly reflected in feeling and behavioral difficulties which retard normal development of both psyche and soma. These detrimental influences are apparently in part permanent and difficult to reverse.

The father's role is not without importance, even though the mother is the key figure. The father is the male exemplar. It is he, hopefully, who gives a masculine flavor to the home and who furnishes the stability and control which every child needs.

Related to the periodic or permanent absence of the father or a male substitute in the father role from so many homes, particularly in deprived and segregated families, many more male teachers in the elementary schools are believed to be greatly needed. The theory offered is that the masculine teacher could provide some of the pattern and the stability for the child that is lacking because of the absence of the father or a male model. The matriarch type of family (mother centered) jeopardizes the boy's role pattern achievement toward a masculine sex role in life.

The father's role as disciplinarian is one factor in the Gluecks' five factors (Glueck, 1960) which predict (where all are lacking) pre-delinquency in almost every case by the age of six. The other factors are: supervision by the mother, family cohesiveness, non-submission to authority, and early evidence of destructive tendencies.

The cohesiveness, or lack of it, of the family is a prime factor in the shaping of character and stable personality of a child. Excessive dependence on television for entertainment is a negative influence on family cohesiveness.

When the television is turned on, the home ceases to be a home and becomes a theater. The family does not talk; they fail to go over the events of the day; they lack support from each other; they fail to communicate. Sometimes whole evenings go by with no conversation (except during the commercials). The family turns off when the television is turned on. Television, if used judiciously, can, of course, be a source of education as well as of entertainment. But children were not designed to sit for hours in front of a little box. Nor should the television be used as an unpaid baby-sitter. The wise parent offers constructive occupation for a child and insists on a reasonable amount of play and exercise. Late shows on school nights should, of course, be out of the question. Some telecasts are clearly excellent. Excessive televiewing is a serious hazard for both the physical and mental health of many children.

Many families suffer from what has been called the generation gap, which is largely a communication gap. Where there is little or no inter-change of ideas, feelings, or involvement between family members, when the home has no cohesiveness, where the parents do not form a workable coalition, obviously any unifying factor in the home will be small and coincidental. The television's effect as a device to mute and even destroy the family as a unit is apparent. When the family does not talk, it does not function as a family. In addition, the television media today is being questioned as to its effect on desensitizing children from the human feelings of compassion and abhorrence of violence, and the possibility of its creating distortions of reality, which, in the view of many, contributes to sick behavior. Reports (Vallance, 1993) indicate disturbed children may be greatly influenced by violence viewed on television, and recent research by the federal government indicates serious incrimination of the excessive violence shown on television is related to many children who manifest violent behavior tendencies. Efforts to limit violence by legal restrictions on media are under serious study by legislators in many places.

It is no doubt true that we can live through our children but not with them. Their world is not our world, and we cannot enter it. The period of rapid social revolution we are now experiencing is evidenced by accelerated changes in dress, speech, and social conventions to a degree not believed possible since the Vietnam era began.

Family control of the child frequently has been replaced by family control by the child. The young daughter does not like the piece of furniture her mother has selected, so the mother takes it back to the store. The teenage boy demands a jalopy or perhaps a sports car to drive to school, and the father promptly goes out and buys one rather than fight the problem. Then the boy spends his time repairing and modifying the car—and his schoolwork suffers. Children are very clever in bringing subtle, unremitting pressure to bear in the direction they wish in order to gain their ends. Parents are manipulated much more than they realize by their children, often for purposes which are undesirable for both children and parents.

The British way of bringing up children has much to commend it—they usually do not ask a child, they tell him. It is well for the family to discuss the various views of family members relative to the purchase of a piece of furniture, the new car, or where to spend a vacation—and adults cannot always be presumed to be right. We must realize, however, that a child is immature, his experiential background is limited, and his judgment is therefore immature and incomplete. Thus, the final decision, the ultimate responsibility, should and must rest with the parents. Until the child reaches his maturity, parents cannot be absolved from their responsibility to hold power of final veto. Too often, parents buy a motorcycle as the last present for a child, on his/her sixteenth birthday. In their later sorrow they realize that it was indeed a last present—from anyone. The number of fatal and permanent disability (amputations) accidents in which motorcycles are involved has increased recently. They might even properly be called murder cycles. Even bicycles are dangerous and call for protective headgear and obedience to traffic laws.

The family may reflect a culture of poverty—or a poverty of culture. Poverty as a way of life is the life program which thousands of inner-city families manifest. Here the vicious circle of the un-people is readily observed: uneducation leads to unemployment, to unhealthy housing and diet and undesirable citizenship (subsisting on relief and hospital charity).

A society which perpetuates a culture of poverty is in part responsible for this triad of poverty, crime, and punishment (which not only does not rehabilitate but instead almost always brutalizes and alienates offenders against society). Punishment for retribution is still justified by many.

Siblings in the family exert a great influence on each other. Birth order is receiving more attention as a personality shaper, with the firstborn apparently becoming, generally, the most successful in life. Rivalries, jealousies, and mutual helpfulness are all possible, and their mixes in daily family interaction are significant in personality determinations.

The psychoanalytic view of the family (Gay, 1988) as a pathogenic factor is undoubtedly important in mental illness. No family can expect to create an ideal environment; traumatic experiences will certainly occur: illness, death, long separation from a parent (as, for example, required by military service), economic crises—and these will leave permanent emotional scars. At the same time, the family can be a foundation for emotional equilibrium and behavioral stability. The almost total absence of adolescent criminal behavior in first-generation Chinese-American families and in Jewish families in the United States is proof of the great control that family cohesiveness can exert.

Family disorganization, disintegration, and psychopathology is commonly observed today. Some claim that three-fourths of all marriages are failures. The divorce rate of one in three marriages is a serious indicator of breakdown of the family in our society. The unfortunate consequences for children of broken homes needs no elaboration. The stresses of urban living are great even with both parents present; when one parent only or the grandparents must do the job, conditions for psychopathology are more likely to be present.

The goal of every nuclear family should be to raise children who will be emancipated from dependency on the parents. This means that support and subsidy for even a long educational period (a legitimate and proper use of family resources) is to be distinguished from continued dependency for hippie living, drug abuse, and drug scene activity. Parental toleration and coddling of adolescent and post-adolescent idleness and debauchery is impossible to reconcile with responsible parenthood. It is as cruel to distort reality for adolescents by overprotection and overindulgence as to fail to support them in school or job training.

The Grecian mean of moderation between neglect and overprotection is difficult to achieve. Perhaps if more errors were made on the side of too early requirement of self-support for adolescents, there would be less trouble. Affluence, providing access to automobiles, liberal spending money, mobility to travel long distances by automobile or air (often on weekends when work or college study is neglected), and tendency on the part of many youths to avoid work—these are definitely related to the social malaise from which many youths suffer today. These same overindulged youths are prone to criticize the establishment and blame their parents and society for their personal alienation and unhappiness.

The family as an economic interdependent entity is rarely found today. The old Russian proverb to the effect that labor is the house that love lives in, is applicable to few families today. Apartment living, early family separation for school and work, and the total absence of work chores at home preclude achievement of the wholesome effects of group endeavor. The rural atmosphere of earlier days where all members of a family, of necessity, shared in the tasks and each member contributed to the very survival of the family resulted in family cohesiveness which has, unfortunately, deteriorated as urbanization has advanced.

Another factor noted in studies of disturbed children is the apparent increasing incidence of emotional maladjustment in the parents. Behind every disturbed child can usually be found a disturbed adult. Parents with marginal emotional adjustments and/or serious borderline psychotic states are unsuitable to guide children. Most psychiatrists agree that schizophrenia is home grown in a social climate of stress and uncertain expectations for conformity on the part of the child. Pill-taking parents often have drug-abusing children. Early diagnosis of incipient mental illness and prompt treatment at this stage is imperatively needed by many maladjusted parents who show various early warnings of personality disintegration such as alcoholism, drug abuse, sexual maladjustment, and work absence or job dissatisfaction.

Suicide, the most frequent cause of death at age fifteen, usually has a preceding history which should alert the family of impending danger. All parents would be well advised to listen to their children, to the subtle cries for help they show. The deep depression, anxiety, and extreme swings of mood which some adolescents evidence should be taken seriously and the child referred for medical and psychiatric help as promptly as possible. Frequently these distress signals may be noted by school teachers or counselors even before they become evident to the parents and should certainly be brought to the attention of the parents. Unfortunately, many of these indications of serious emotional breakdown are not taken seriously by the associates of the sick person. It is evident that many parents are completely deceived by their children who are on hard drugs; a fatal overdose may be the first warning signal they receive.

The most common failure of parents is inattention or lack of concern for adolescent problems.

All families experience ambivalent feelings of love and hate. The same father who can buy a new automobile for a son or daughter must, at times, take away the keys as a result of improper use of that car. Parental abdication of their inescapable role playing, however, is deplorable. The family as a viable social organism is threatened today. Let us hope its defects are corrected before we see the family disintegrate as an institution.

The thrust of this chapter is its recognition of the salient power of the family to mold socially adjusted children or, regrettably, to produce depraved and degenerate predators on society. Each child is an omnibus in which all of his life experiences and ancestry ride, and which each day is reshaped to cope with life, for better or worse, by living experiences.

Chapter 4

THE PUBLIC SCHOOL

In contemporary America, the school is a social institution that serves some 64 million students and costs about $484 billion each year. During the past fifteen years, it has been fashionable to cite the school as an institution in serious trouble. Actually, schools today have for the most part begun to change, to adapt to the deep changes in society itself, and school personnel are doing a better job of educating young people than ever before. The twelve-year educational ladder, which used to begin at ages five to six and end for most at seventeen or eighteen, has expanded in many cases to an eighteen-year ladder beginning with age three and ending with an associate degree at a community college. More than half of those of school age will graduate from high school after more than twelve years of free education. No other country can come close to those figures. Also, American secondary schools have more students in proportion to their population than any other country; education is America's biggest business.

Schools are in the process of revitalization and redirection after years of "bashing" by officials and the news media that began in earnest with "A Nation at Risk." For a decade, most school personnel took the abuse quietly while inside they were thinking, "My students are learning more and are better able to meet the challenges of today than students ever were in the fifties in spite of the fact that there is much more to learn with technology so rapidly expanding the availability of information, in spite of the breakdown of the family as we knew it then, in spite of the violence that constantly bombards everyone through television and newspapers, and in spite of an increasingly available supply of drugs."

The Seven Cardinal Principles of Secondary Education (U.S. Office of Education, 1917) are still applicable today as we look at what schools are being called on to provide: command of reading, writing, and mathematics; health; worthy home membership, development of ethical character; worthy use of leisure time; vocational training; and citizenship. Later, international understanding was added as an objective. Today, in addition to teaching all of those things plus the use of the tools of technology (computer literacy, laser disks), schools are called upon to teach children how to cooperate and collaborate in the work place and even to provide basic nurturing and nourishment that many parents are unable to give beginning when the child is an infant.

Caving-in by school administrators, unconcern and disinterest by many parents, burn-out by some teachers, and disaffected and violent youths of school age have created a critical situation. Combine with those problems attacks on the schools by *economy-first* reactionary groups who think first of saving tax money and last about quality education, by *School Choice* groups who want to be able to spend their tax money to support private schools that teach their particular religious and moral, and by *Home School* and *Charter School* movements with individuals who often want to begin their own school in their own home or garage to keep their children from having to associate with people who are "different" from them and the crisis increases. "Voucher schools" will doubtless soon be declared unconstitutional.

Privatization (paid for by tax money grants as vouchers to individuals or private school entities for free parental choice of schools), home schooling "yard kids" by parents (with risk of social learning objectives not being met), and video instruction also under non-public school auspices are being tried. All have serious possible defects when compared to most good public schools with a structured, sequential curriculum, taught by certified teachers and administrators in schools with physical facilities for athletics, music, art, and recreation.

Private schools for elementary and secondary education financed by tuition are costly, elitist (not all parents can afford them), and a threat to free public education which loses the financial help and interest such parents could be devoting to public education. States reimburse local districts per capita each day the child is in a public school. The push for private school support comes from some parents who believe a greater degree of local control of schools may be preferred to state-mandated curricula, methods, and materials for instruction. Others want a school that will foster their own religious beliefs which, of course, is a reason currently forbidden by state and national constitutions.

Children are bringing guns and knives to school *and using them.* Others come to school "stoned" on alcohol or drugs. Girls are having babies at age 11 or 12. We can now look back on the times when the major problems were girls who wanted to go without bras and boys who wanted to wear hair that was below their shoulders and wish our current problems were so minor. The problems of today's youth are deeper than the topics of protest their parents engaged in; in basic ways, many schools today are very different from those that today's parents attended. In this context, it is necessary to look at what has been happening with schools as they, with society's help, have embarked on the process of change:

1. Traditionally, the school has not fitted well to the child. It has usually forced all to take a standard curriculum which does not relate to the needs and abilities of many. It is a *word* school rather than a *doing* school. More than a hundred years ago, Professor John Dewey wisely stated, "Children learn by doing." Such is the case now with hands-on science activities, the use of manipulatives to teach math, the increasing requirements for student writing, and the availability of computers as tools for learning and for developing real world products. Vocational education is changing from home economics and agriculture courses to work-force specific training designed to prepare students for the jobs that are currently available as well as for jobs that no one at this time can envision. Community partnerships set up so that students can learn firsthand about businesses and industry in their area are flourishing. Requirements for "coherent sequences of courses" for ALL students that will insure preparedness for the student to pursue either continued education (through a company's training program, a community college, or a four-year university) or for entry into the work force are being instituted in high schools around the country.

2. Children are not born equal—they are born grossly unequal in physical and mental characteristics and into homes and societies which are grossly unequal, born into an environment of social asphyxia. In the past, schools have treated all—except for special education students—as being equally capable of learning. This has been a great error. Recently, many schools have expanded their services into homes where poor families are not able to provide experiences that lead a child to readiness for school. Parent trainers work with the child and the parents beginning, sometimes, as soon as the child has been born so that the child (when he or she finally enters school) is ready to learn what the school is there to teach. Parents who are themselves illiterate or

who are proficient in a language other than English are being encouraged (or even mandated) to take adult education courses so that they will better be able to help their children succeed in school. Expanded days, Saturday school, summer school, and year-round school (with interim classes for students who need more time) all are options that schools are increasingly embracing as they work to provide quality education for all of their students.

3. Students who were born physically or mentally handicapped were automatically sent to "special" schools or special classes within schools. Many of those students are now being included in regular classes with the help of special education personnel who collaborate with the regular teacher to insure that all benefit from the experience. For instance, Down's syndrome children are now able to participate in regular school classes and to succeed. Also, with the help of technology, many physically handicapped students including those who are born quadriplegic or deaf and blind are now able to communicate to the point that they can graduate from college with advanced degrees if they choose to, and they can go on to lead productive lives. On the other end of the spectrum, most schools now provide recognition of and opportunities for their gifted and talented students to keep them from the boredom that "more of the same" yields and to challenge them to use their God-given abilities productively. Although many students are still dropping out of school because the curriculum "does not relate to their needs" as they see them, there are fewer students dropping out of school each year as schools become increasingly able to recognize and deal with students who are at risk of dropping out. Many schools are now also offering "drop-in" opportunities so that people who in the past had dropped out of school can return and earn a high school diploma.

4. Schools have been institutions in the total sense of the word: impersonal, authoritarian, rigid, and mechanical. They became that way thanks in part to the industrial society during which and for which they developed. The goal of schools during the industrial age was to produce people who were fitted for the assembly lines, people who could do "cog jobs" that called for endlessly repetitive tasks to be accomplished without question, without creativity, without deviation. As a response to society's need, schools themselves became factory-like with students taught from the out-

set to stay in line, sit in straight rows looking at the back of the person in front of them, soak up what the authoritarian teacher was presenting, and perform tasks that called for rote memory and regurgitation of facts. When society changed to the information age, schools as institutions were slow to change for several reasons, among which were the lack of money to purchase technology and retrain teachers not only to use the new technologies but also to teach students to locate information rather than to memorize it, to work cooperatively with others, to share ideas, to communicate ideas and information effectively, and to be creative in addressing problems for which there were no clearly right answers that had yet been determined. School facilities (many of which are still in use) provide perfect symbols of the industrial age schools and embody the reasons why schools were slow to change: desks are still bolted to floors in rows, and bells tell of class beginnings and endings.

5. Today's violence, drugs (Covey, 1992), and sexually transmitted diseases are out of control, in part because the schools failed to see these changes and did not cope with them effectively at the start. Too many educators joined with society in general and put on blinders to what young people were doing. Still today, some people are saying there is not drug problem in their school or in their community. The handgun problem is a barometer of the school's atmosphere, where discipline has been neglected. The school is not the cause of the problem, but it suffers from society's tolerance of illegality. Guns are a plague on today's America. There is no reason why handguns should be accessible to minors; there is no reason for schools to tolerate instances of guns on their campuses. At this time, many schools are developing Zero Tolerance policies that call for students to be arrested immediately for any assault or battery regardless of the student's age, ethnicity, gender, special education status, or family wealth. There is also a growing awareness on the part of school personnel that violence begets violence, that educators themselves need to model ways to deal with anger and frustration that do not encompass physical or emotional abuse.

6. Public support for free education for "all the children of the people" has never been adequate. Dual systems of education for whites and blacks has been costly and has brought up generations of black people who have had inferior schooling—this cannot be

denied. In addition to the African-American students, there have been increasing numbers of Hispanic and Asian children to the point that in some places, Caucasian students of European ancestry are the minority. This shift from white to brown majority places demands on a society not used to dealing with people of color. Integrated schools have been functioning successfully in many places, but physical integration alone has not been enough to insure equity when it comes to educational opportunities. All too often, schools with high populations of African-American or Hispanic students are poor schools with limited resources. Equitable funding must be insured for all students if integration is to bring a free education for ALL children of this nation. School personnel also need multicultural training so that they can, in turn, help their students accept the wide variety of people who now inhabit our "global village" called school.

7. Educating students about sex (Kinsey, 1948) (pregnancy and sexually transmitted diseases like AIDS), drugs, social problems, and personal deportment is something that schools still are not doing very effectively, mainly because the society that governs schools is still ambivalent to say the least about what should be taught to students in the way of personal decisions and the development of moral values. The pervasive and destructive influences of violence and the distortions of reality on television must be countered by sensitivity training, readings, and involvement among persons who care. The ghetto of the inner city with its social asphyxia must somehow be redirected with hope and opportunity, including better jobs and housing. To the extent allowable within various communities, schools have been working to address social and moral issues. They also have been, in many cases, concerned about the business of developing a community of caring within the school itself, recognizing that in many instances school is the only place where children can learn how it feels to be accepted, to be loved. The world abounds with stories of students from extremely poor backgrounds who were "saved" by a caring teacher who reached out and touched the student's life.

8. Where a child lives should not be the determining factor in the quality of his education; ignorance cannot be quarantined—the *un-people* move from their ghetto surroundings to other areas and take with them their ignorance, superstitions, and hostilities. Recent

tax reform proposal seeks to ease the burden on property owners for school tax support. The goal should be to tax the money needed for schools where the tax base is, for children where they are. The present tax system is clearly unfair and inadequate, with the suburbs able to afford better schools with less tax load than the inner city or rural areas.

The school has been called the place where we polish the brickbats and dull the diamonds. To learn should be a natural activity for children, as it is for monkeys. Unfortunately for many children today, the *school turns them off* or makes *pushouts* by its methods and materials for learning. The child is confirmed in his self-image of unworthiness. The self-fulfilling prophecy of many students and teachers results in a child not making progress. Too many teachers and parents expect too little progress from children who have built-in handicaps of poor home environment, absence or enriching experiences, poor school equipment and staff (as goes the teacher, so goes the school), and uninspired school authorities who are content with the pedestrian quality of the teaching system.

The school itself can contribute to poor mental hygiene for many children by its unreasonable expectations of progress, failure to adjust to individual differences, and rejection of many children who do not readily conform to hypothetical *norms*. Many schools are now addressing those problems by increasing the amount of learning time available to students who need more time and/or providing an ungraded primary setting where students are allowed to move through, for instance, the kindergarten, first, and second grade curricula as they are ready.

Mental maturity testing (IQ) is subject to many limitations of reliability and validity. Its findings must be interpreted in terms of whether the test is culturally fair and what kind of "intelligence" exactly it measures. IQ tests based on reading are reading tests, not valid tests of mental maturity. Mental maturity tests have long been criticized on the grounds that they are not *culture-fair*—they fit relatively well only to Western, white middle-class children for which they were designed and normed. Black or Hispanic children are clearly at a disadvantage in such testing. Children receiving special education services are often found to be misassigned and are, in fact, able to succeed in the regular classroom with little or no extra help. Added to those problems with analysis of student abilities is the recent work of such people as Howard Gardner and David Lazear (*Seven Ways of Knowing,* 1991) on multiple intelligences showing that intelligence as it has been defined through the tests of mental maturity encompasses only two of seven ways that a person can be a "genius." In fact, everyone has strengths in at least one of the seven "intelligences."

A school is a lot of books—and, recently, computer links to books—with a few good people around to help get something out of books. The Instructional Media Center or Multimedia Center is the beating heart of every school. Children must be taught to read and then they must be motivated to read. There never was a good reader who did not read a lot or a poor reader who did not read at all. There are three ways for people to learn to read: read, read, read. A wealth of high interest, low level reading materials have developed over the past twenty years, thus providing the means of motivating students. Strategies such as DEAR (Drop Everything and Read) and reading/writing workshops have increased students' opportunities to learn to read by reading. The trend away from isolating reading from the other language arts of listening, speaking, and writing has also increased students' abilities to become effective communicators both of oral and written language.

School is the "business" of adolescents. How the school does its job is critical to social progress and delinquency control. Ghetto schools must have superior staffs to offset deficiencies for learning which exist there. Society's problem is not whether we can afford good school; the question is whether we can afford *not* to have good schools. The very existence of society as we know it depends on quality education for all, regardless of residence or economic factors. Those who oppose free public education or who seek to divert public education funds to private channels may be advocating a dangerous course.

Public support for non-public (parochial, private, or even home) schools has been increasing in the past few years and drugs and violence in the public schools receives more and more publicity. Many people feel that some subsidy is justified, but constitutional provisions which require separation of church and state forbid such help at this time. Performance contracting involving contracts between private companies and school board authorities has recently been judged to be less than a success, although this idea is still being tried in several areas of the country.

Little doubt exists that there is a direct connection between money spent for schools, the socioeconomic status (home environment), quality of school program, and the achievement of pupils both in school and post-school. Schools must be funded by tax dollars. There is an intolerable disparity between rich and poor school districts which state laws have created by refusing to equalize tax money generated within school districts. Children should not be penalized for the accident of their residence's location. Every child of a state deserves quality schools. A child has only this day to be educated. If he is cheated, each such child and society will surely pay dearly. Ignorance cannot be quarantined. Later remedial efforts can never be a full or satisfactory restitution to that child or society.

The funds required to provide a quality education must be available to all schools. Districts wishing and able to finance a superior school program can and should be encouraged to do so; this must be, though, in addition to a quality basic state program. Where does your state rank in this connection?

A state income tax patterned after the federal income tax would appear to be an equitable method to pay for public education. Sales taxes, local real estate taxes, and user's fees are regressive taxes. They are a greater burden on the lower-income people. Efforts to ease the tax burden on low incomes are receiving more attention by tax-setting legislators in 1995. It is unfortunately true that some people do not believe in quality education for all the children of all the people. They fail to realize the costs of permitting social asphyxia.

Education should be a lifelong process. The unfavorable improverished home environment of many pupils is recognized today as a grave handicap in life's race for success, for it often entails psychological settings of poor motivation and reduced expectations.

In many of the nation's largest cities, half or more of the pupils are non-white and preponderantly poor. One out of every three of those students drops out of high school; the average pupil who stays in school is two years behind the national reading norms. Many teachers and pupils live in constant fear of robbery or injury from physical assault; police officers must patrol school corridors to protect teachers and pupils. *Compensatory education* —designed to offset the built-in cultural disadvantages of ghetto children—is in the process of being changed from a separate program for specially identified children to a source of revenue that can be used to improve the effectiveness of instruction for all students with the idea that if the entire campus is improved, the opportunities for students at risk of dropping out of school will improve. From the 1930s on, so-called *progressive education* has called for the school to be fitted to the child, for the school to adjust expectations of school achievement to the capacities of each child. What many educators are now discovering is that children can often do much more than the school has recognized or demanded of them up to this point.

Deprived and segregated environments of millions of culturally different children destine them to poor academic progress and early dropout if the school does not accept their differences and work to meet their needs. These children will be the last hired and first fired in employment shifts and will comprise our prison, relief, and non-paying hospital case loads. A *tax-eating* status is a certainty for most of them. How long can a democracy survive with such long-term, costly liabilities clearly inevitable unless the present collision course with social disaster is averted? A total mobilization of the nation's resources is imperatively needed to cope with the imminent disintegration of today's society.

Apparently we have a choice between supporting public education as it must be supported or of pouring infinitely greater sums of money into a police state tomorrow. The loss of human potential—which is the greatest waste of any natural resource—with its concurrent tragedy of escalating welfare costs, crime, and social asphyxia is directly related to ineffective schools.

Children attending public schools who are proficient in a language other than English (PALS) often are reading several grade levels below their chronological or school age cohorts. Bilingual education where students are taught in their native language as they're learning English has been a help for many students who live in areas where there are many people who speak the same language (like Spanish or Korean), but because all schools are basically reading schools, students who are poor readers are destined to fail, to drop out, and to fill an inferior life position. It is estimated that two and a half million Americans have reading handicaps and that over eighteen million adults cannot read well enough to fill out *survival forms* —applications for Social Security, drivers' licenses, Medicare, or bank loans.

A great fault of many schools is that the teacher talks too much and the children talk too little. Some ninety percent of the talking should be by the children; the teacher does not need *recitation* practice. Children will *learn to do by doing* as Professor John Dewey taught at the turn of the century, not by being *talked at* by the teacher. Our Armed Forces in World War II used multisensory aids as the method of teaching; they *kept the talk short.* The pattern of instruction, with emphasis on the *doing* was *tell them how, show them how, and have them do it.* Passive learning is not good learning; the learner must be active and involved in *finding out.* Schools can be exciting places of discovery. When they are not, when children are *turned off* as is the fault of some of today's mechanized, impersonal schools, society suffers. Misguided school boards which cut support for guidance counselors and special education teachers in economy actions are surely compounding delinquency and life adjustment problems for future great costs to society.

The first step in the educational process should be the assignment of teachers who are psychologically adjusted and emotionally sensitized to working in an environment where slow, sometimes hostile students are the rule and not the exception. This facilitates mutual trust and understanding. Secondly, programs must be developed to place the student in classes that are adjusted to his learning capabilities and preferred learning style. More emphasis needs to be placed on teaching students to problem solve, to work cooperatively, and to communicate effectively as they are being prepared for jobs that currently do not exist since technology is changing so rapidly. Slipshod work, absenteeism, and substance abuse can no longer be tolerated on the job. We have for too long sent a boy to do a man's work.

Students also need to be taught the psychological moral values of the society in which they can probably expect to live and work as well as the mores of other societies in today's shrinking world. The language and accents of the social class in power economically must be taught if employment is to be expected in today's working America. Multicultural studies contribute little at this time to job placement or success. What happens, though, when African-Americans or Mexican-Americans become the power brokers? As the minority becomes the majority, this could well become the case.

Discipline is necessary if a stable learning environment is to exist in our schools. Unfortunately, methods used to this end have traditionally been negative in nature. Corporal punishment has happily, for the most part, been replaced by suspension practices. These practices, while they do temporarily remove a problem from the school, have manifold adverse aspects. Disruptive or habitually truant students are the least likely ones able to afford a further void in their educational experiences, although they usually welcome the vacation. Lack of supervision by parents increases the possibility of the suspended student's becoming involved in delinquencies within the community at large. More effort must be directed by the schools toward providing more positive means of maintaining discipline, thus avoiding shortcomings inherent in the exclusive employment of negative reinforcement measures.

Many schools have turned to using In-School Suspension (ISS) as one means of disciplining students. Within the ISS is often found a learning specialist and a counselor so that students needing help for whatever reason can receive that help. Alternative schools are also being established in many communities so that students who were formerly labeled "incorrigible" are now being provided with a differently structured environment—another chance to complete their high school education. Usually the alternative school uses alternative methods and materials to meet the needs of students who have not been reached by the traditional school setting.

Children having children is a national disgrace. Until recently, though, pregnant students were treated as contaminated outcasts and banned from the campus when their pregnancy became evident. Those girls were penalized at least a year of their education and most never returned to regain the lost educational opportunity. Now, most schools allow students who are pregnant to continue to attend school as long as their doctor permits; if health prevents them from attending classes, schools provide (by law in Texas) a homebound teacher until the girl is able to return to school. Many schools are also providing day care for the babies (often with the help of high school students so that they can learn parenting skills) while the mother returns to complete her education. Even with these support systems, many young mothers continue to drop out of school and later join the surging welfare rolls. A final way to help these people is beginning to be set up now with welfare office workers starting to collaborate with the schools and with adult education offices to provide educational opportunities for welfare recipients.

Unless the public realizes the crucial importance of the public school as the great (but not the only) shaping force it is and gives the school as a social institution the means to do the tremendous task assigned to it, the waste of our most precious natural resource—our children—will continue its dismal course with social disintegration the inevitable consequence. When teachers are paid at least as much as truck drivers and school is viewed with the respect it deserves, then perhaps a better life will dawn for all of us. Churchill has said, "Civilization is a race between education and disaster." Time is rapidly running out. Continued work to improve the schools and to support its increased role in preparing people for tomorrow's world is imperatively needed.

Chapter 5

PEER GROUPS

The family constellation is the setting for the intra-family turmoil manifested in the hostility, the difficulties, and in the lack of cohesiveness of many families. However, the family constellation is not the entire social milieu of our adolescents; for some it is the weakest influence in later years of this period. School, peer groups, the neighborhood, and organized social agencies, such as the YMCA, Boy Scouts, Girl Reserves, church, and, regrettably, delinquent gangs also may shape in part this course of development.

* Probably the most potent control over an adolescent is his peer group: only a very brave youth will deviate from the norms of his own fellows. This subtle control is pervasive and thorough; it operates on both conscious and unconscious levels; moreover, it is especially powerful during the late adolescent years.

The word peer means an equal, one having approximately the same age, education, and social standing. A high school graduating class is considered a peer group. The class of a military academy is a peer group. A group of army or navy recruits, or a police academy class, where they may or may not be in residence in barracks yet really get to know the characteristics of each of their colleagues, is a peer group. An additional important consideration is the power of the group in creating a group consensus, which sets standards of behavior and values and compels compliance.

Part of the explanation of peer group control is the psychological defense mechanism of identification. The individual feels insignificant and powerless, but by joining with his peers he shares a sense of their collective power. If this power is shown in mass action—such as a protest march—there is a feedback to strengthen his feeling of belonging. When he wears a costume similar to others, he feels identification; his own weakness is lessened and he may even feel omnipotent, as do mob members.

Another explanation (also a defense mechanism) is projection. The individual feels his deficiencies, but by blaming others, as in a bigoted racist group, for even more serious defects, he is able to minimize his own faults in his own eyes. Hence, he feels less insignificant and better adjusted. However, when there is systematic or prolonged reliance on both identification and projection, incipient mental illness may be present.

The peer group sets standards of conformity which apparently derive from mass consensus and follow-the-leadership of some exemplar—a charismatic or personable individual who is accepted by the group as arbiter and authority. This leader may be a star athlete, physically attractive, or it may be a freak, such as Charles Manson, who sets his own peculiar requirements for members of his family and who compels absolute conformity. In any event, the peer group results in a relatively homogenous closed circle of in-group members who show solidarity and give group support to members. The police as an organization show marked adherence to peer group controls. This may or may not be beneficial to society at large.

Children in play groups both fear and obey; they are fear-controlled from the first time they are placed with other children. The most frequent behavior patterns are accepted and it takes a courageous child to deviate in any way from this pattern. Modern psychology plays down fear as a desirable form of social control; prompt reward for desired behavior (Dr. Skinner's Reinforcement Theory) is much preferred.

The flower children (or freaks as they are currently being called) are an example of a peer group in operation. The first characteristic of his hang-loose culture is the uniform: baseball cap worn backwards, baggy, oversized clothing, earrings (both boys and girls), headband, beads, long uncombed hair, sloppy attitude, and neglect of personal hygiene. These counter-culture types are exposed to skin infections, rheumatic fever, hookworm infestation, pediculosis, malnutrition, neglect of dental hygiene and epidemic social diseases. Sexually transmitted diseases are common, with HIV/AIDS a new plague since 1985.

Today's youth in its extreme swings of mood seems almost psychotic— that is, out of touch with reality. Unreasonable demands are made for early total freedom from personal responsibility for behavior which may even be criminal in nature, such as truancy, drug abuse, arson, guns, and throwing stones at police. Youths plead that they have the right to do their own thing, without regard to the social or personal consequences of their deviant behavior. It is true that their behavior is judged to be deviant by the square or straight adult society; however, without the labor and organization of this square world, these youths would not be clothed or fed. Their behavior is criminal when they violate laws and harm the person and property of others; their adolescent status is clearly no excuse for felonious and heinous acts. Juveniles today (ages 12–15) are increasingly regarded as requiring to be handled by adult court standards. Curfew laws are being enforced with good results in many cities, an innovation since about 1992.

When groups of peers meet and rationalize ("rapping" is their word for it), they seemingly are able to convince each other of the propriety and legitimacy of their decisions. There are increasing numbers of youths who conform to the way of life, with their style of dress and nonconforming life (drop out from school, avoid work except in extreme need, nonconformism such as camping out under bridges and cult harems, (such as the Branch-Davidians in Waco) and support for liberal welfare social programs and more public financing of job training.

One must hasten to recognize that the deviants to whom we refer in the foregoing paragraphs represent a small percentage of the total youth population. The great mass are attending schools and/or working with dedication. Those who show deviant behavior, however, are vocal and visible. More than half of American youths are in our colleges or pursuing vocational goals today and are not attracting attention by exotic behavior; the small visible minority of youthful dissidents create a false impression of today's youthful numbers.

The youthful offender shows the negative attributes to a more pronounced degree than the youthful nonoffender, and in addition he acts out his unconscious motivations; he shows marked impairment of ego control; his ability to adjust his gratification to reality is minimal. He acts often on impulse at the moment, with little or no conception of the consequence of his acts. He wants his gratifications now, not in an uncertain future.

Many youthful offenders apparently have been conditioned (brainwashed) by the feedback effects of their antisocial life cycle to respond negatively to unusual social controls. Many have found that they win by delinquent acts oftener than they lose and are punished. This finding must, of course, reinforce their sociopathic behavior. Too often, deviate behavior is rewarded (as evidenced by the position of leadership granted to cult leaders or the misfit by some youth groups) and socially desirable behavior may not be reinforced, and even perhaps discouraged. We have perhaps given youths too much chance to say no. This may well be attributed in part to the vicarious sense of fulfillment derived by the members of the herd when the leader does that which the individual youths do not quite dare to do alone. Mob hysteria has long been recognized as a powerful force in criminal acts.

Gang affiliation (Covey, 1992) is still a serious police problem in inner-city areas and even in small towns. The gangs survive year after year with new leadership and recruited members. The leaders are described as possessing considerable leadership ability and their continued position as leader depends on their judgment and authority. Some of these gang in recent years have become extremely vicious; homicides are frequently reported from their rumbles, in contrast to a generation ago when fists were used instead of zip guns or knives. Discipline is strictly maintained by the leader. The common view of gang members appears to be conviction that their conduct is right because it is held to be wrong by the larger society around them. The following quotation from Thrasher (1968), written two generations ago, applies equally to today's gang member:

> He breaks up a party, molests school children, taunts women and girls on the streets, engages in petty thievery of personal belongings. He is a vandal. It gives him pleasure to despoil and destroy property wherever the opportunity arises. He does not hold a job. Being a loafer, he is often found on the streets or in poolrooms. He idles away countless hours in smoking, gambling, and rough horseplay. He is always ready to ferment a brawl but seldom willing to engage in a fair fight unless backed by his pals. He is coarse and vulgar in his talk. In totality, he is a thoroughly disorganized person. (p. 66)

This is the hoodlum. He is a young member of a gang whose demoralizing influence easily promotes criminal behavior. However, if he remains with the gang and the process is not checked, the end product will inevitably be a seasoned gangster or professional criminal, if he survives turf warfare. Drug sales finance gang activity in various vice actions.

Peer group controls are a phenomenon. Suffice it to say that some young people today are not particularly fearful of parental approval, or that of the clergy, the police, or of the school authorities. Students may not be afraid of school authorities—but they surely are afraid of those in their immediate entourage, those with whom they associate. It is characteristic of the young to conform, to avoid any unusual dress or behavior, and to guard against any deviation which may earn them the label of chicken.

The milieu in which a youth moves, his peer group affiliation, is a potent shaper of his philosophy of life, his school relationship, and his conformity (or nonconformity) to the expectations of family and society. Differential opportunity to be exposed to influences which lead to integration of his personality, or to its disintegration, shape the individual to a marked degree. The kind of peers he associates with—whether they are eccentrics, antisocial, and even delinquent, or straights, who are upward mobile and accept deferred gratifications to achieve a future goal—is believed to be highly significant. Parental pressures on youths to change peer group membership is often futile; environmental manipulation, where possible, is one partial solution in some cases. In this connection, some form of national service (military or civilian) would appear to have much merit in neutralizing millions of youths ages 17–19 who now fill our prisons and halfway houses at great cost.

Some neighborhoods are prone to have much more exposure to delinquency-generating influences than others. If the non-school hours are shaped by gang activities, if the street is the milieu, one can reasonably expect the learning feedback to be less than ideal. Many thousands of youths who have dropped out of school, who are unemployed (and this is many times higher for nonwhites than for whites), and who see around them exemplars who have made it—criminals, drug pushers, and deviates—are led to believe and accept as fact that crime pays.

For college youths, fraternities and sororities offer in-group status and self-esteem to the members. These Greek societies are not without negative aspects on college campuses, however. There is a great deal of rivalry among the groups, and the lines of social class distinction are perhaps nowhere as finely drawn as they are among the various fraternities and sororities. Academic excellence is a fraternity goal on many campuses, and the experience of living in a peer group has values which may and do contribute to success in later life.

The youth unconventional subculture provides group sanction, symbols, and support for the way of life which has become common for thousands of nonconforming youths, not only in the United States, but worldwide. Notable exceptions are North Korea and Red China, where such freedoms do not exist. Thanks to parental subsidies and society's permissiveness, today's social revolution has not succeeded in winning popular support.

Representative of the drastic changes in society are the voting privileges in local elections extended in some states to the 18–21-year-old group; extreme styles of clothing (or lack of it); revised (and perhaps abandoned by some) sexual standards; and more license in speech, movies, television, and the press—actually bordering at times on hard-core pornography. Youth protest has affected national politics to some extent, with major political parties making an all-out effort to win votes of youths.

Many have observed that some of the goals of todays youth are indeed laudable and proper: the fight against consumer abuses, the war against pollution, the spotlighting of the anonymity and powerlessness of the individual when confronted by monopolistic corporations, in favor of the civil rights, anti-war, disapproval of the extinction of wildlife and abuses of conservation, less materialistic goals, concern for the poor, and the expressed horror concerning man's inhumanity to man.

That youths do not coincide in their views with the older generations (twenty years is considered a generation) is not new to the world; that youths can effect the far-reaching changes which have occurred in recent years is new. The political clout of the 18–21-year-old voters can be significant, especially in local elections where large student populations may outnumber permanent residents.

Peer group control is not, of course, limited to the young. We have peer control in our standards of personal hygiene. In the United States we have a generally higher standard of personal hygiene than in most developing countries around the world. To most of the people in the world, the sanitary way of life is almost unknown. In some Asian countries, all running water is believed to be pure. There it is not uncommon to have toilets emptying into a stream, while downstream that same water is used by people for drinking and to wash their dishes and clothing; soap is almost nonexistent; scalding water is rarely to be found; potable water itself is in short supply. But most of the people have the same standards for that particular area.

In conclusion, the power of the peer group is impossible to underscore too heavily; it is relatively independent of parental, school, police or church control; it is highly flexible and unstable; it must be recognized for what it is: a phenomenon of today's social revolution which must be respected and its effects at least recognized and hopefully understood by all who interact with youths. To this end, encounter groups (rap sessions) for parents and children, and students and college authorities, can help sensitize both youths and adults to some of the problems of adolescents. Such communication channels should hopefully have been open from early childhood. There is a patent need for programs on how to be a parent. The consequences for failure of adults to relate meaningfully with today's youths could be disastrous to the perpetuation of society as we now know it. Clearly, today's youths will be tomorrow's adults and power figures. In time, they will mature, but in the interim they cause many criminal acts. Alexander Pope:

> Vice is a monster of such hideous mein,
> As to be hated, needs but be seen.
> But seen too oft, familiar with her face,
> We first endure, then pity and last embrace.

An experienced police officer has commented relative to changes in his personal attitudes as a result of this course and text: "I have come to understand especially in the chapter about peer groups why my sons wear their hair longer than I like it. I can also now understand that the snarling, spitting, sneering youth is emitting signs that delve far deeper into societal problems we adults face and have to cope with than his dislike for me as a person and as an officer."

The reader will hopefully realize the power of peer group pressures on youthful offenders. We must hate the sin, not the siner in interactions, not adversarial, judgmental or confrontational—a difficult task, admitted.

The peer group, 1995, with lethal dangers is the organized gang, as found typically in less affluent neighborhoods. Police are needed to monitor halls for assaults and use metal detectors to prevent weapons possession inside premises. Gangs now resort to lethal handguns for drive-by shootings and intimidations, with frequent serious incidents. Vehicle thefts are common, related to drug traffic. Drug sales near schools are often observed. Carjacking and vehicle thefts are common.

Chapter 6

SEXUAL RELATIONS

Sexual behavior and its many social manifestations is a pervasive and powerful force for both healthy personality shaping and its disintegration. The intimacy of sexual outlet forms causes it to be a fruitful source of deep emotional turmoil and maladjustment. No other form of human behavior is as vulnerable to defective expression as is sex.

Doctor Freud (Gay, 1988) placed sexual motivations as a key factor in his psychoanalytic theory. In brief, he believed that personality development and efficient human behavior throughout life were dependent on resolution of powerful instinctual sex drives and their later-life expression in socially desirable forms. To him, the human animal was primarily moved in behavior by sexually related deep personality factors which were formed and structured by both genetic and environmental forces and largely were the result of very early life experiences centering upon relationships with parental figures (his Oedipus and Electra complexes). Infantile sexuality was the source of conflicts and neuroses, in Freud's opinion.

There is ample evidence today that sexual themes dominate advertising, drama, speech, films, television, styles of dress; the pitch of motor vehicle sales (a girl draped over the hood of a convertible) clearly proves this point. We are indeed living in a sexual revolution: books, films, magazines, and television have had almost complete relaxation of the censorship standards prevalent as recently as a few years ago. Dress styles and colors reflect this change; perhaps the word psychedelic (or mind-altering) best describes these changes we all notice around us.

Adolescents are approaching the peak of sexual potency and these hormonal drives have great physiologic force. These motivations contribute greatly to the storm and stress of the adolescent years. An adjustment involving socially approved satisfactions of these powerful drives must be somehow achieved, or their expression in serious antisocial behavior will almost certainly result.

For some adolescents this process ends in failure to reach orthodox typical heterosexual identifications and relationships. These cases are labeled deviates or perverts, yet their form of sexual outlet may, for them, be satisfactory and rewarding. Recent social rethinking relative to unorthodox sexual outlets is in the direction of more tolerance (for example, homosexual relations between consenting adults in private is not a crime in England nor in several states in the United States of America).

Heterosexual adjustments are a form of learned behavior. Where the environmental shapings have been distorted by parental modeling, learnings from the peer group, and/or institutional living (e.g., prisons), the result is observed to be a much greater incidence of homosexual outlets. It is the considered view of most authorities that homosexual behavior is almost entirely learned and is almost never genetically determined. Some homosexuals can be conditioned to a heterosexual pattern; however, others do not appear to want or to be capable of changing. The life space of homosexuals is not usually conducive to their continued happiness; jealousy, fleeting liaisons, absence of a cohesive family relationship, and even violence, are often noted, with poor prognosis for later-life interpersonal adjustment. The condition is diagnosed, as are other forms of sexual perversion, as evidence of gross ego failure; the deviate is usually unable to relate satisfactorily to orthodox heterosexual outlets. Some genetic involvement is suspected.

It is believed that homosexual behavior is in part the product of parental shaping: the boy has no real mother to relate to and the girl has no real father figure to help set her life pattern. In addition, the learnings in a homosexual environment reinforce latent unconscious homosexual drives which most individuals possess without awareness on a conscious level. Lasting heterosexual adjustments are very difficult to achieve for many couples. As stated above, the degree of intimacy and emotional involvement is extreme in sexual relations. The delicate balance of psychological and physiological factors required makes maladjustment of sexual outlets most difficult to avoid. When immaturity and emotional blocks, such as from frigidity and impotence, are present, serious consequences involving incompatibility and hostility are sure to be present. Some estimates set the proportion of marriage busts at 75 percent, in terms of lasting mutual sexual satisfaction.

The psychopathic deviations of sexual outlets, such as forced perversions and criminal assaults, clearly involve degrees of mental illness and should be regarded as belonging in a medical (psychiatric) context and not, as is usually done, in a criminal or court setting. Criminal behavior may well be involved; however, possible mental illness of the accused is a fact which must be recognized. Some psychotic sexual deviates are potentially dangerous and some should doubtless be confined for life; others may, with psychiatric help, be perhaps restored to society and become taxpayers rather than tax-eaters. Early indications of serious sexual deviations among adolescents should clearly be regarded as warning signals, and prompt referral to mental health authorities is imperative. Early treatment of all mental illness, including sexual deviancy, is extremely important; such cases do not get better spontaneously; on the contrary, they almost always get worse if permitted to continue untreated. Psychosis involves loss of contact with reality, and long-term care in maximum security is indicated for such patients, with poor prognosis for life adjustment.

The need for early (junior high school is too late) sex education is obvious, as evidenced by childhood pregnancies, the epidemic rates of sexually transmitted diseases, ignorance of facts of basic physiology, and divorce rates running about one in three marriages. Many juvenile-age marriages are highly vulnerable to failure, related directly to the psychological immaturity of the couple. The tragedy is that basic ignorance of physical and psychological facts is often the direct cause of marital incompatibility and unhappiness. Inadequacies of sexual performances are rarely physical; the trouble is not from the neck down, it is from the neck up.

Sexual promiscuity is often related to acting-out behavior. The girl or boy is ventilating hostility against parents or society; the boy wants to prove his masculinity by fathering a child; the girl seeks popularity or money and clothes otherwise denied. Such unconscious motivations are most often found in immature, insecure, distorted and neglected home environments. The relation of welfare to sexual dysfunction among juveniles is receiving much attention today on national levels. Substance abuse is a serious causal factor in sexual dysfunction and vice.

Low family income (poverty levels) is a potent shaping force, as already discussed. Where parents are unable to relate meaningfully to their children, for whatever causes, sexual deviations from societal norms often are evidenced. Where the home does not reflect mutual respect and a coalition between husband and wife, where fighting and violence are often present, deviate behavior is the norm for the children in that home. There is little doubt that the counterculture is based on the satisfactions which members get from sexual freedom, substance abuse, and belonging to a peer group (a sense of family) which they did not get, or thought was lacking, in their home setting. Cases of welfare abuse are often reported, and the costs of dysfunctional homes with the cycle of poverty unbroken for generations is causing much concern, particularly in New York where the governor in 1993 declared a campaign of reform.

It is estimated that some four to eight percent of males and perhaps two percent of females are predominantly homosexual; some of these are bisexual, with both male and female partners at times. These high percentages mean that there are millions of homosexuals in the country. Some relation of homosexual behavior, sexually transmitted diseases of HIV/AIDS spread, and crime exists, with cases of homicide and blackmail related to homosexual behavior often not reported. In general, homosexuals are not inclined to use violence. Their activities seldom come to police attention, for obvious reasons: their activities are victimless, interpersonal relations, unless minors are involved or force or threats are used.

The relationship of prostitution to drug abuse is well known. Some four hundred to five hundred dollars a week is needed to support a heroin addict; to get this much money by working is not possible for addicts—crime must be the solution for them. The pitiful cases of addicted prostitutes are shocking. Children of addicted mothers are born with physical addiction, and irreversible harm is probable.

The Kinsey Reports (Kinsey et al., 1948, 1953) of the mid-1950s drew back the curtain on the American bedroom. The ten thousand cases of both male and female respondents revealed many startling and hitherto unknown facts relative to human sexual behavior. Difference in types, frequency, and psychological factors in sexual outlets were identified for social classes. Subsequent research studies have shed additional needed light on this extremely important aspect of human behavior, with research currently being continued (Kolodny, 1994).

For many adolescents, the formative years are a cruel jungle of rating and dating, cars, clothing, athletic competition (to make the team), scholastic stress (for college eligibility), and attempts to remain a member of the in-crowd.

Some parents pressure their children into early dating and adult-type social relationships. This forced hothouse environment is doubtless hazardous for many children, particularly as it relates to sexual aspects of immaturity.

That adolescent sexual behavior is fraught with hazards for both sexes is clearly evident. Tragedies of extramarital teenage pregnancies, venereal diseases, abortions, and related suicides are commonly reported. Sex is a force of the most violent power; to fail to give sexual motivation its due is to deny reality. A rational understanding of the role of sex in contemporary American life is imperative for all. Doctor Freud's creative genius has indicated the tremendous and pervasive scope of human sexuality. A frank acceptance of this fact is needed, together with education to unmask ignorance concerning sex.

Full-blown epidemic venereal diseases are rampant worldwide today, with the youth counterculture particularly vulnerable and infected. Ignorance and misinformation is a shocking aspect of this grave threat to the nation's health and well-being. The irreversible consequences of untreated syphilis and gonorrhea are debility and invalidism and include sterility, blindness, psychopathy, and early death. The spread of HIV/AIDS in Central Africa, Haiti and elsewhere is a worldwide catastrophy.

That today's youths hold many distorted ideas relative to VD is obvious; abysmal ignorance of the physiology, psychology, and biology of sexually transmitted diseases (STD) are, together with similar ignorance concerning drug abuse and contraception, major tragedies afflicting youth. Knowledge taught by schools during late grammar years and early junior high school years is imperatively needed. Unfortunately, misguided parents and school authorities often fail to see the great need for sex education, sex hygiene, and family planning instruction. The consequences of such ignorance is catastrophic for many young victims and for society in general. To delete the benefits of scientific enlightenment from the school's 1995 curriculum is indefensible today. HIV/AIDS must be given full treatment in both elementary and secondary schools: nature, transmission, and control.

The question relative to the origins of homosexual behavior, whether it is a product of abnormal biology or is the result of sexual socialization, cannot be answered definitively; doubtless both nature (genetic endowment) and nurture (environmental shapings) operate in unknown proportions with any individual's development. We are each of us the product of heredity and environment as shaped by social conditioning.

Clearly contingent or non-contingent reinforcement by feedback cybernetic (circular causal) chains from which goal-seeking and self-controlling forms of behavior, may emerge. Life's experiences are related to all human behavioral patterns, such as alcoholism, drug addiction, fetishism, enuresis, transvestism, obesity, psychopathic and criminal behavior, and including homosexuality. Apparently a failure of proper conditioning has occurred.

Aversion therapy using pictures, slides, electric shocks have had some success in changing some homosexuals to heterosexual patterns. Some individuals are intermittently bisexual, with partners of either sex preferred at times.

Recently, militant homosexuals have struck out at the discrimination, humiliations, punishment and harassment of which many people express toward homosexuals. These militants allege that society is wrong in forcing homosexuals into the role of an oppressed and discriminated-against minority. They say this makes the homosexual a revolutionary, along with oppressed and militant groups like blacks, Hispanics and women. They say homosexuality is assuredly no advantage, but it is nothing to be ashamed of, no vice, no degradation; it cannot be considered an illness. They consider it to be a variation of several functions produced by a certain arrest of sexual development.

Chapter 7

JUVENILE VIOLENCE

In considering mental illness in adolescents, we should first differentiate between those few who are manifestly full-blown psychotic, living in a dream world, from those who, although perhaps severely neurotic, yet are in touch with reality and have insight into their personality maladjustment which is less than wholesome. This is a fine line of distinction, but the criterion to differentiate between these two categories is that a neurotic individual retains insight into his condition, whereas the psychotic individual has lost this insight and is functioning in a cloudy, unreal world, to which he may retreat when threatened by stress related to emotional or organic causal factors.

Persons who have lost contact with reality either temporarily or for longer periods of time must be regarded as severely mentally ill. Such individuals are indeed sick, and closed-ward inpatient treatment (institutional care) is indicated for them until they have recovered sufficiently to care for themselves in a protected environment, which, hopefully, will be followed in many cases by restoration to mental health. Although such individuals may be found in public school situations and on our streets, they are, in fact, beyond the capabilities of the preventive and treatment facilities and procedures which are usually available to police, corrections, and social rehabilitation. Accordingly, in this presentation, we will concentrate rather on the child who exhibits abnormal behavior, but still is in touch with reality in more or less some degree.

Children respond to environmental shaping, to love and security or to the neglect or violence which they may experience. We know that more children die from the battered-child syndrome than die from the total of children's diseases. Many children are killed everyday by parental and custodial abuse. The shocking case of Susan Smith in South Carolina who drowned her two children in December 1994 is one of many such children killed by parents. (The first suspects sought in missing-children's cases are the parents.) Those who survive are indelibly marked, psychologically as well as physical, and these emotional scars may be grave handicaps for many children as they seek personality integration through the adolescent years.

Lack of cohesiveness of the family means that the family is a fighting society rather than a supportive society—the child must actually strike out even to get some bread with peanut butter on it. When a child is brought up in this kind of environment, he will find, long before he is six years old, that he can solve his problems by striking out, by taking what he will not get otherwise. He finds that this pays off for him; by operant conditioning, it is reinforced. He has satisfaction when he fights, strikes out and hurts people. Since he has never received love, affection and security, he cannot experience these feelings; therefore, he grows up cold, dispassionate and vicious. Unquestionably, the psychopathology of early childhood begins in such a distorted environment. The first eighteen to thirty-six months of life are believed to be critical in this shaping.

When children are thwarted, they respond routinely by striking out. We can expect a certain amount of unreasonable acting-out behavior. When this becomes vicious and a pattern, obviously it shows marked abnormality. Much of this overt behavior is the result of unconscious motivation. The child is striking out in overt behavior for reasons which he does not understand. An example would be the child who steals something, then as soon as he gets outside the store throws it into the garbage can. Another example would be the child who runs away from home for reasons that he cannot explain, but which clearly are the result of overwhelming stress, of the predisposing experiences and psychological trauma which the child has had, which lead him to respond by antisocial and sometimes even criminal behavior. Over a million runaways are reported yearly.

The fact of unconscious motivation cannot be denied. We are each of us at any time the result of the shaping psychological and hereditary forces which have brought us, with social conditioning, to what we now are. These shaping forces begin very early in life, in the first weeks and months, and we never forget them. They are indelibly recorded in our nervous systems. This is proven by the facility with which they may be recalled under hypnosis, by open brain surgery, by dream analysis, and by free reverie. We actually record in three dimensions and in color everything that happens to us, even long before we have words to express it.

• A certain amount of hostility is natural for children. Children of tender ages do not use words to express their hostility; they strike.

However, the child soon begins to use words. This build-in hostility is one of the key ideas of Freudian theory. Egocentricity, the id, this seething cauldron of our emotions, is part of our primitive ancestral inheritance. Actually, we are covered by a thin veneer of civilization—a little bit of drugs, a little bit of alcohol, a little fear, a little sexual arousal, and the individual becomes a vicious animal. He is not concerned with anyone but himself, as is shown in mass panic catastrophes where crowds trample others to death seeking to escape from fires, sinking of ships, and in war hysteria. Mob hysteria during lynching is an example.

Perhaps to expect man to live in a civilized way, considering the short 15,000 years or so we have been even partly civilized (in terms of the 1,750,000 years or longer that man has existed in relatively his present form) is to expect the impossible. The consequence is that the children will show hostility. We must expect them to show it. In fact, the child who shows no hostility is a sick child. But when a child seizes upon hostility as his *modus operandi* for solving most of his problems, obviously he is crossing over a line of demarcation and demonstrating a need for therapy.

The school situation is one which we must closely scrutinize, because there we often judge children in terms of adult standards. We expect all children to perform equally—but nature and nurture did not make them equal. They were not made equal by inheritance nor by their environment, and when the school attempts to set the same standards for all children, it is flying in the face of reason. We must set our standards of achievement in terms of the capacities of the individual—and this is done very rarely in the typical school. This is not entirely the fault of the school systems. The schools are like a child who has been sent to do a man's work. We have teachers who are burdened with forty or fifty children in a class, and a teacher in that situation *keeps* school; she cannot *teach* school. Overemphasis on the academic curriculum is criticized today; manual training is clearly more appropriate for many pupils who are now forced to take academics or leave school.

We may be in danger of total catastrophe in our schools because the children are not being reached individually. The reports of indiscipline are increasing everyday; policemen have to be stationed in schools; and the result is a learning climate which is nothing short of disgraceful for this richest country in the world. The question is not whether we can afford to have good schools, the question is whether we can afford not to have good schools.

The school (see Chapter 4) becomes an intolerable place for many children and they respond by running away from it. It is too painful for them to endure. They cannot endure to have other children laugh at their poor progress. Peer group influence, as previously noted, is responsible for shaping behavior more than anything else. Youngsters do not worry about teachers, parents, or even policemen; they do obey and fear—very greatly—the children of their own social group.

Truancy is an indication of the failure of the schools to meet the needs of children. It is related in part to the poor home background that some of these children come from: an environment where education is not prized, where the models they see are those who are making it in drugs, vice, gambling, and other crimes. The whole example they see is negative as far as social values are concerned. In the ghetto, criminals are often the generals in their society, not the failures.

Children learn early that if they throw themselves on the floor and kick and scream for an ice cream cone, the mother runs and gets a dime for them—so they continue this pattern. The reinforcement they get from their behavior is such that they continue to manifest it. This requires, certainly, that mothers must be taught better child-rearing practices. The tantrums described above are an early indication of the acting-out violence that seriously maladjusted children show. The child growing up where standards of reasonable behavior were not set and required and who finds he can achieve satisfaction by deviant behavior, will likely continue it.

Early inability to get along with others is a criterion noticed immediately by teachers, social workers, and others who handle juvenile predelinquents. A tendency is shown by disturbed youths to force the external world to conform to the individual rather than for the individual to conform to the external world. This may be an indication of pre-psychotic behavior or of severe neurotic behavior. If the child is in a home where unreasonable standards of conformity are set, where there is rigidity, where there is frequent corporal punishment, where the child feels insecure, helpless and unwanted, obviously he will not develop patterns of behavior that will enable him to get along with others. We must question whether such children would be considered normal. We know there is going to be some mild indication of all these traits, but where they become marked, where the behavior is obviously maladjusted, then clearly some therapy, some search for understanding of the behavior is indicated.

Can such abnormal behavior be handled within the family? It is almost hopeless to expect that it can be handled within the family unless the family has been given some help by way of prior educational opportunity to learn something about human behavior and human relations. In a home where there is illiteracy, where the mother is an alcoholic or an addict, or where there is a succession of uncles living in the home (the father having long since abandoned the family), it is futile to expect that the parents can do much by way of therapy for deviant behavior. This situation is found often in minority ethnic and lower socioeconomic classes, but exists everywhere. Here the school must again extend its resources to cover this unmet need to teach mental hygiene, citizenship and ethical character.

Home visitation by the social worker is desirable. If the mothers could be persuaded to come to a class, perhaps held at night, where they could learn something about home economics, family planning, dietetics, personal and mental hygiene, and child psychology, the present deplorable situation could be, in time, improved. For example, if mothers would learn just the one simple fact that children under the age of two or two and-one-half do not have sphincter control and cannot voluntarily control bladder and bowel functions, many children might be saved from beatings and even death because they become wet or are soiled. Just a little knowledge of physiology is needed, so that the mother would understand that she is expecting something from the child which he cannot control until he has physically matured enough to have this voluntary control over the sphincter muscles.

On a long-range basis, we know how this can be handled and should be handled—that is, by having a first-class educational system everywhere; children could be given education for day-in and day-out living. For example, sex education should be given during the elementary school years, when sexual experimentation begins. We must get away from the prudish idea that children in junior high school are not going to get pregnant or contract VD. We know that they do become pregnant—thousands do, and VD is epidemic among youths, and, today, the specter of HIV/AIDS is a terrible fact demanding attention. Somehow the school must teach these fundamental facts of life, since it seems the home, and church, and non-school agencies are ineffective in too many instances at all levels of society. It does not matter much whether a child can spell if he doesn't understand the basic facts of life relative to personal hygiene, sexual functioning, and some insights into interpersonal and intrapersonal human relations: mental hygiene.

The family itself must have an emotional climate of security, support, affection, respect, and discipline, which will enable the child to come to school and to learn efficiently. Too many children are on the streets until midnight, go to school without breakfast, and have no one to care whether they have clean clothes to wear or a bath every day. We must somehow mobilize our total resources across the board for physical care, health care, and emotional and mental care. Our children deserve better.

The immediate need on the part of the family would be to have an intervention of ideas by visitation counselors, who would concentrate on such simple things as just making sure that a child gets to bed at night by a reasonable hour on school nights; that non-school hours are supervised by some responsible adult. The family must be sensitized to the fact that great harm and trouble is in store unless each child is treated as someone who is important and is given proper supervision and care.

Where the home has fallen apart so completely that this supervision is impossible, even with the help of social services, then certainly a foster home or institutional care is the only other answer. Much more use should be made of foster homes in preference to institutional care. Environmental manipulation in some cases must be resorted to. The child must be taken out of an environment where he is destined to become a prison statistic, into one where he has some hope of adjustment. A 24-hour school may be the answer for some children. Lately, some people advocate institutional care (not orphanages of the past) in preference to the gross neglect offered in some so-called homes.

When overt hostility regrettably results in a police charge, the matter is brought out into the open. If the family cannot handle the child, or the family is dysfunctional, he must be handled by others with more capability. A child who is incorrigible, who is a delinquent, who is a runaway, must somehow be controlled. If this means institutional confinement, reluctantly then this must follow, under proper professional auspices. We do not want Dickens' style orphanages to be models.

Where intervention is clearly indicated it must be implemented. To hope that troublesome cases will spontaneously get better is a serious misconception; they usually get worse unless treated.

Individual violence occurs almost invariably at a stress point where something has triggered off the violent behavior. The violence is an acting out in the face of a frustration, or a block to some satisfaction, or there has been a buildup of anxiety of a compulsive nature and the normal controls have failed at that moment. There is a heavy emotions coloration of the episode. We must bear in mind that we think emotionally—we don't think with the whole brain. We think with the hind brain, the old brain. The forebrain, which is a more recent acquisition of mankind, functions when we are calm and collected. But when we lose our cool (and we actually do lose it, because the temperature goes up), "condition red" happens. There is sweating, rapid heartbeat, deeper breathing, more sugar in the bloodstream, the whole physiological reaction which accompanies anger. Violent behavior is related to anger and to fear. The triggering of this can be a very mild stimulus, or it may take a tremendous concentration of stimuli to bring the individual to the flash point. Violent behavior is a blind striking out, where people use their hands or use instruments to hurt or kill. Unfortunately, guns are often available.

Violent behavior is sick behavior. The individual, after the violent episode, will usually have regret, but not always. Some psychotic individuals can take a life and have no remorse. These are totally psychopathic, sociopathic individuals. But the violent episode which has a pattern of occurring shows that the individual has been using this as his solution. This is his *modus operandi* and he seizes upon it as a solution when he finds other alternative solutions are not available to him. He will then strike out in desperation.

In order to prevent a pattern of violent behavior, we have to try somehow, particularly in early childhood, to condition children that violence is evil, that it is counterproductive, that it does more harm than good, that it does not solve any problems, and that it is often irreversible and may cause permanent harm. It is an unbelievable animal reaction which many manifest. This requires a whole reshaping relation to our childhood, adulthood, and an understanding of what fear, anger, drugs and alcohol will do to release inhibitions and make possible violent, vicious, depraved behavior. This is what happens when an individual acts under blind stimulation of loss of rationality. He acts on a gut-level basis—and the results are often nothing short of catastrophic.

In this connection, incrimination (correlation) of violence on TV with violent acting-out behavior by some children is accepted as a plausible theory by social psychologists today. Violent behavior is almost a normality for some.

Although any one-to-one correlation of heredity and criminal behavior in a particular case is clearly not possible, it is believed that genetically influenced variables may exert a thrust toward criminality. According to Doctor David Rosenthal of the National Institute of Mental Health, brain-wave abnormalities associated with bad judgment and poor impulse control; low IQ; mesomorphic body build with low tolerance of frustration and poor ego control; psychotic and pre-psychotic behavior related to a genetic factor; chromosomal abnormality manifested in psychological distress and personality disturbance; alcoholism and drug addiction with an inherited predisposing factor; abnormal sexual behavior related to genetic factor; and hyperactive children with inherited factor, are recognized as shaping forces which affected behavior, whether criminal or non-criminal in manifestation. This is not the same as saying criminals are born to be that way; rather, it is to admit that genetic factors must be considered as part of the nature-nurture combination already discussed elsewhere.

Bill Moyers' seminal report on his travels over the United States looking for solutions to the escalating violence among gang people today as reported in *Parade* (*Houston Chronicle* 8 Jan 1995) have been of great interest to this writer: The tragic personal experience which led to his search and the successful programs he found in communities, churches and schools across the nation were documented in two powerful PBS TV specials broadcast January 8th and 10th, 1995. His "tips" picked up from talking with activists, experts and young people themselves all over the country are available in a 20-page booklet that describes model violence-prevention programs. Write to *WNET Community Resource Guide* for "Act Against Violence Guide," Dept. P, P. O. Box 245, Little Falls, N.J. 07424-0245.

Chapter 8

SUBSTANCE ABUSE

In this brief condensation of a many-faceted problem, the news reporter's five questions will be used: who, what, where, when, and why.

Who: Substance abuse in 1995 includes narcotics (marijuana), alcohol, tobacco (snuff, smokeless compounds), over-the-counter pain pills, legal (prescribed) injections, pills and self-medications. Pharmaceutical products are not all harmful, of course, but misuse of some over-the-counter items does occur, with toxic results. We are a nation of pill-takers. Young people are largely poorly informed relative to medicines they ingest without medical supervision.

What: Recently, cocaine products processed into "crack," "speed," and other forms, have become the addict's drug of choice and have disastrous results for countless naive users who may be "hooked" after even a brief experiment. Nicotine's addictive power has been proven.

There is little doubt that the extent of drug abuse is much greater than reported. Parents and teachers are deceived; police cannot identify and charge many users; and society seems almost helpless to cope with the problem. Adults show an unbelievable incidence of substance abuse. Tranquilizers are taken daily by millions of people, in addition to diet pills and pep pills. We are indeed a nation of drug users. Apparently the idea has taken hold that there is a pill to solve every problem of life; ingestion of drugs without medical supervision is commonplace, and there is apparently easy availability of drugs to all levels of society. In this connection, some believe punishment for users of heavy drugs is a viable next step in control. Also, some interest is being shown today in decriminalization of narcotics (Trebach and Inciardi, 1993). Like alcohol abuse, which led to Prohibition, perhaps over-the-counter availability of drugs would take away the profit which the criminal drug underworld lives on. Whether narcotic drugs should be legalized is debated today. Arguments pro and con are made by responsible professors and scientists. The experience of national alcohol prohibition from 1918–21 has been less than promising. The chemical desires of Americans, according to

Vallance (1993), create grave dilemmas for society. Until personal ethics, family values, social trends, cultural role models, education and religion are radically changed and the daily life-style of millions of Americans made less stressful, with perhaps less pill-taking and self-medication with over-the-counter nostrums, substance abuse will be unmanageable.

A new wave of aerosol inhalants is reported in 1995, with gasoline, paint solvents and sprays widely used. Teenagers have little comprehension of the grave risk they run, nor can they explain the physical effects of sniffing deadly fumes which brings on their "highs"—the heart stoppages and irreversible brain damage similar to asphyxia.

The same ignorance leads to many deaths from inhalation of smoke during sleep in house fires. Smoke alarms are not present in many poverty-level dwellings, although required by fire codes. Often a cigarette in furniture or bedding is the source.

All medicines and drugs are toxic when ingested in quantities not medically prescribed. Alcohol is by far the greatest abuse problem, with millions of alcoholics and countless so-called social drinkers in this country. The costs of alcoholism are astronomical in terms of industrial accidents, motor vehicle accidents (over half of all fatal motor vehicle accidents involve alcohol), loss of workdays, and health deterioration related to chronic illness and early death. Access to alcohol, beer notably, for minors is inadequately controlled anywhere, it seems. High school and college binge drinking is epidemic. Nicotine is by far the greatest health threat and has killed more people than all other drugs combined.

Other drugs abused are the narcotics (cocaine, heroin, morphine, and marijuana) and tranquilizing barbiturates and stimulating amphetamines. All drugs have the potential for causing addiction and/or psychic or emotional dependence. Their use, except under medical supervision, is dangerous and illegal. Their prescription by a physician for therapy is, of course, medically approved for depression, weight loss, narcolepsy, Parkinsonism, insomnia, and as an anesthesia for pain.

Where: Drug abuse occurs at all levels of the social scale, at all ages (even neonates are born addicted), and throughout the world. Certain countries which are the chief suppliers or processors of illegal drugs are finding that many of their own young people are drug abusers; this is helping to bring pressure on authorities in these countries to prohibit all drug production (particularly the opium poppy). Southeast Asia, Asia Minor (Turkey) and Latin America (Columbia, notably) are well-known centers for drug traffic. The United States government is now subsidizing farmers who formerly grew opium poppies in certain places in order to eradicate, as far as possible, the production source. This has had little success. How the U.S. government can sell tobacco worldwide and at the same time subsidize tobacco growers with public funds is difficult to understand. We warn of health dangers on tobacco products, yet sell those products to smokers to their manifest dangers abroad. This is nothing short of disgraceful and destines millions to ill health and death, thanks to profit-seeking Americans and other tobacco-producing countries.

Apparently, ghetto areas for large cities are most involved in drug abuse, but its spread to affluent suburban areas is now a fact, creating problems for many middle and upper-class families.

When: The epidemiology of drug abuse has shown a dramatic rise in rates since 1960. The Vietnam War created a special problem of hard-drug addiction among returning veterans. This may be the most costly fallout of that war. There has been a rise in drug addiction following every war, including the Civil War of 1861–65. It was, ironically, the treatment of morphine addicts among Civil War veterans that led to widespread use of heroin. In 1898, it was discovered that this new wonder drug was able to keep a morphine addict from suffering withdrawal symptoms and was thought to be non-addicting itself. It was four or five years later before it was learned that heroin was four times stronger than morphine and at least twice as addicting. Today, some ninety percent of the narcotic addicts are on heroin.

All authorities agree that recent figures of drug abuse show alarming increases in both relative and actual incidences of drug abuse in this country and worldwide. Youth culture worldwide apparently has embraced drug abuse and cigarette smoking as its trademark.

Rehabilitation (abstinence) from abuse of hard drugs is estimated to be about fifty percent among those who stay in a clinic's program; for those who attempt to kick the habit on their own, the rate is thought to be two to eight percent success over a three-year period. The rate of cure may be only one percent.

Why: Multiple reasons, many specious and irrational, have been advanced relative to why drug abuse occurs. A simple explanation would appear to be this: people take drugs because they get something from it. A chemical cocoon is sought to envelope the abuser and to shield him from the real world from which he flees; the real world is too threatening, too painful, and he cannot cope with it. Drugs enable him to cop out.

Some few individuals become addicted after medically prescribed use, but most addicts admit they graduate from alcohol or mild drugs to hard drugs (some eighty percent of addicts begin with marijuana).

The grave likelihood of permanent addiction evidently does not deter experimentation with drugs. That a pill or bottle can become master of one's life is not realized by many addicts until they are hooked. Less than one percent of hard-core addicts are estimated to be ever rehabilitated—a dismal prognosis indeed and in itself sufficient reason to dissuade any experimentation. As with alcoholics, each day is a test whether drugs will win out; recovering alcoholics is the term used by Alcoholics Anonymous—it would apply certainly to drug addicts, who really are never cured until dead.

Most authorities agree that addiction is related to personality: some individuals from a combination of constitutional factors and social conditioning life experiences seem particularly prone to psychic dependence; the craving for drugs is initially psychological, rarely in response to physical needs. The problem initially is from the neck up, not the neck down. Sedation or stimulation, with euphoria or a feeling of well-being, and escape from reality is the effect from drugs. Obviously, efficient functioning in today's competitive and aggressive society is difficult, if not impossible, for most drug addicts. Most drug abusers are diagnosed as of marginal personality integration; drug abuse is a symptom of their mental or emotional illness. They have one common characteristic: they feel they cannot function even on a low level of performance without the crutch which drugs provide for them. Drugs are often abused in a social setting with others who are seriously maladjusted and in rebellion against the square world. This aspect of drug abuse and the counterculture nature of the drug-abuse-set adds a serious complication for many youths.

Some addicts apparently have adjusted to their habit and function with relative success while continuing a controlled form of abuse, working and masking their addiction at the same time. Employers are attempting to identify these persons through medical screenings, and labor unions are trying to fight for this problem, since "high" employees may be dangerous around machinery. Urine samples are diagnostic of many kinds of drug uses and should be used more widely in screenings for employment.

Juvenile drug users are especially vulnerable to peer influence; many will experiment with drugs in order not to be "chicken" and in order to belong to the crowd. The turbulence of adolescence, requiring many adjustments of both psychological and physiological nature, has been covered in previous chapters. The thrill aspects of drugs, their forbidden nature, and the mistaken idea of many adolescents that they can take or leave drugs, are factors to be considered. That a felony conviction for drug abuse can be a lifelong handicap is apparently disregarded by many youths.

Fatal consequences of experimentation with heroin, glue, aerosols or other solvents, LSD, and other bad trips seem to be of little or no deterrence to others. An abuse-prone individual will often continue on from mild to severe drugs until he is a confirmed drug user and the road back is virtually blocked.

Contrary to popular belief, few adolescents are introduced to drugs by big-time pushers—peers do it. The myth that the pusher is usually a long-haired bum has no basis in fact—a peer group member who sells to maintain his own habit is by far more common.

In contrast, the adult abuser of drugs commonly has a history of personal and social maladjustment. He is a loser in life's race, and the chemical curtain which alcohol and drugs provide is too rewarding for him to reject.

The ghetto with its segregation and deprivation is a natural habitat for drug abuse. When the pressure is too great from environmental and/or emotional stresses, the drug abuser will retreat to the detachment from reality which drugs provide, no matter what the cost or the resulting eventual aggravation of his problems. The fractured and fragile family patterns often seen in the ghetto are both the result and cause of the instability of that world of the street. However, addiction is in no sense restricted to over the tracks.

The cost in dollars to maintain an addict is estimated to be from $150 to $300 or more per day. Few people can legitimately earn that much money, and crime would be perhaps half eliminated if profit from drug traffic ceased. Robbery, shoplifting, burglary, forgery, assault, drug traffic, and prostitution are the usual crimes associated with drug abuse. The inner city is the target area for drug traffic control; the underground of the criminal worlds is its medium for operations. The millions of dollars changing hands daily in organized crime operations is the lifeblood of drug traffic. Its eradication will be most difficult. A mobilization today of the nation's public health, social and educational agencies is imperative. As of 1995, success is little or none in terms of drug prohibition.

A final word relative to marijuana: this drug is not believed to be addictive, yet it produces a form of intoxication that can result in unpredictable and occasionally violent behavior. It is legally classified with the narcotics for the purpose of control; chemically it is different from the hard narcotics. In about one-third of the states, the laws do not distinguish between marijuana and the harder drugs, such as heroin and cocaine. Penalties are harsh for possession (perhaps two to five years) and for sale (five or more years). First offenders for possession or use are often treated more leniently. Today there is a two-year minimum penalty for federal marijuana violators—the same as for heroin violators. New bills in the Congress would allow judges to use their discretion and no jail sentences would be required. They would also allow first-time offenders to have their convictions eventually erased from their court records. These less drastic penalties are being recommended by legal, prison, and health authorities.

New classifications of each drug are needed, depending on its (1) potential for abuse, (2) acceptance for medical use, and (3) the degree of dependence (psychological as well as physiological) it causes.

Controversy surrounds the no-knock provision laws which would allow police to enter a house on a specific court warrant without first knocking, to prevent disposal of the evidence. At this writing, the provisions of the law, in the opinion of many police officers, make it difficult to obtain convictions for possession of narcotics, when pushers have an opportunity to destroy evidence prior to the moment of search.

A major peril from pot smoking is its stealthy engendering of apathy, altered life goals, and false concepts of reality, among frequent users. Pot is today ten times more potent than formerly. Pot is a lung irritant, similar to nicotine in tobacco in its effects.

While it is true that many of the youngsters who experiment with marijuana will go no further than the experimentation stage and may come to no serious harm as a result, a significant number will. The so-called soft drug users, once they are introduced to the drug subculture, find it all too easy to continue on to hard drugs. The problems or attitudes which brought them to the experimentation with marijuana in the first place are not solved or changed by its use—indeed, may be amplified. And, unfortunately, rarely will an adolescent admit or acknowledge that there is any likelihood of his getting hurt or that there is any danger involved in his trying the various drugs. Thus, treatment or the halting of participation in the abuse of drugs in most cases presents a great many obstacles. Until and unless the adolescent is motivated in a direction away from drugs, the path downward is is steep and sure.

Since the general topic of drug abuse first merited inclusion in a text dealing with the psychology of the youthful offender—approximately 1968—the attention which now must be given to it has taken a quantum jump. Let no reader be deceived as to the deadly serious effects of drug abuse as it threatens the very core of our social order today. We are in deep trouble.

If Americans are becoming increasingly drug dependent, is there any relationship to the more than $1 billion plus being spent every year to advertise over-the-counter and prescription drugs? Four of the five top network TV spenders are drug companies. Drug use is two to four times greater (two billion prescriptions each year) than in some other countries which seem to have the same general level of health. Perhaps it is no coincidence that drug abuse is now rampant in its first TV-raised generation.

Vallari (1994) believes that drug use may lessen with "comfort from improvements in other realms of behavior such as peer and family relation, reduction in proneness to violence, better self-understanding and self-esteem."

Clearly, an orientation of the values of our social order is imperatively needed: a philosophy of life which is rooted in humanistic values, of work ethic, of morality, and of respect for health and life. Unless this can be achieved, the continued existence of society as we know it is in jeopardy.

Punishment for repeated illegal use of drugs is believed by some to have merit as a necessary step in control with severe penalties for repeat offenders or dealers. To lock up a kid selling crack and to let the purchaser off free defies reason. The purchaser is an accessary before the fact, it appears. Some believe first-time teenage offenders should be treated as "respondents": their incarceration, if needed, should always be in a non-criminal restriction of freedom with the goal of rehabilitating, not retribution, and eventual return to full citizenship without stigma for most "respondents" who show evidence that better adjustment to life in the free world is possible with them. Shock treatment with juveniles confronted and taunted by long-term hardened inmates is being tried. "Boot camps" are in operation in many states. These innovations show promise in the direction of less-mandated long prison terms. Five-year incarceration has long been recognized as a great hazard to return to free world crime-free adjustment.

Chapter 9

PUNISHMENT AS SOCIAL OBJECTIVE

The quotation: "Punishment as therapy is semantic acrobatics" is an excellent master sentence for this unit of *Psychology of the Youthful Offender*. The Old Testament idea of dire vengeance for wrongdoing, of an eye for an eye, or spare the rod, spoil the child, is today believed to be not only antedated but even viciously harmful in its counterproductive aspects. The purpose of correctional action is to correct; it is not to make the offender less adjusted and more sick. To hate the sin, not the sinner, must be the goal of judges, parents, police, teachers, correctional officers, and social workers.

To punish is to harm; it is not in any sense curative or restorative; it is upside-down thinking. Punishment does have a partially effective immediate deterrence value; at the moment—for that instance of behavior—it is of some value as a control. It does not, however, get at the root cause or causes of misbehavior. It does not change the root causes; in fact, it may make these basic causes more potent as negative harmful shapers of behavior. For example, the felon who has "paid his debt" by prison time may feel he is now at liberty to commit more crime.

The child who is slapped may feel he has been absolved of his responsibility for that behavior. He may not have internalized any learnings from the punishment other than that he hates the punisher and that he will be more careful not to be caught in the future.

This is not to advocate a regime for any child that is free of controls. Children must be trained to accept and expect the appropriate consequences for their actions. A child not out of bed in time for school will be tardy. This usually puts him in an uncomfortable position. The rationale for family rules may hopefully be explained to young children (ages four to eight), and, by use of operant conditioning with reinforcement only for desired behavior and physical punishment abandoned, children may be inducted, with help of great patience and forbearance by elders, into responsible self-directed social roles at home, school, and society. The underlying causes of garden-variety antisocial behavior may well be

74

some mild degree of psychopathology, distorted reality from childhood exposure to criminogenic factors, inability to succeed at school or to earn a living (no trade, illiteracy, low mental and emotional maturity), physical and/or mental defects which are rarely if ever diagnosed, and with remedial measures neglected or absent.

Conformity and compliance based on fear only is worth nothing. A police department whose members obey regulations only when superiors are present has no real discipline. Control which is not self-control and self-motivated is a sham. No supervision can be always present. Hence, the goal must be to instill the abstractions of duty, honor, dedication and moral suasion, not the specific corrections of punishments, sanctions, and psychological or physical trauma.

The results over the centuries of the indiscriminate use of punishment have been dismal. Man has not become better as a consequence of the most barbarous and inhumane punishments. He continues to show his animal-like, vicious nature, as at Auschwitz. In fact, he is only papered-over with civilization. Physical blows, confinement, psychological blows (derision, scorn, invidious comparisons, vicious demeaning criticism) are severe and often counterproductive. They decrease the self-control potential of the involved person, lessen his self-confidence, damage his self-image, and confirm his lessened status in his peer group. "What others think of me, I will think of me, and what I think of me, I am."

This is not to say that some psychopathic individuals must not at times be confined ("sick" persons who are mentally ill, depraved, degenerate, or defective). Some must be permanently removed from open society for their welfare and that of others, when their capacity for self-control is inadequate. A role remains for constructive criticism and psychological controls—children should be guided by operant conditioning, to shape behavior in socially desired directions. The egocentric and selfish hedonism we show at times must be guided by rewards, non-rewards, and, in some instances, by rational punishment (for example, a fine for a moving traffic violation). However, the children who misbehave the most are invariably those who have been beaten the most. The other extreme, where no effective control has been used and internalized, is equally to be deplored and results in seriously maladjusted individuals who are consequently unfit to cope with life's problems.

In interpersonal punishment there is the involvement of the punisher, usually in an emotionally angry setting where he has lost his cool. When we are not calm and collected, we think emotionally with the so-called old brain; the new brain, the reasoning area of the frontal areas of the brain, is short-circuited. This accounts for the unreasonable, irrational acts we perform under emotional stress and which we look back upon by saying, "I must not have been myself." In these instances, children are maimed and killed (more children are killed by their parents than die from childhood diseases), and many violent acts of homicide and assault result. Some so-called police brutality undoubtedly is related to loss of cool in provoking situations (some excessive use of force does occasionally occur in police or corrections work, but such behavior is punishable and is decried by commanders). Brutality against the police is common; one in every ten police officers is assaulted each year. This gets little or no publicity by news media.

The punisher cannot wear two hats equally well. The parent who buys his son a new bicycle is also the one who must at times take away its use when necessary. The punisher in his role leaves emotional scars which cannot be erased. This predicament teaches that punishment which is in retribution, to get even, or to ventilate displaced aggression (for example, the father loses his job, beats his son that evening for a minor infraction) is dangerous and always counterproductive. The punishment does not correct the root cause for which punishment seems to be in order at that time. The punisher gets some emotional relief by his displaced aggression, and the physical act of administering the paddling does ventilate his frustration, but at a high cost to both himself and the weaker subordinate second party. Children do resent greatly the use of superior physical power by adults to force compliance. Parents who use corporal punishment beyond the early few (perhaps age three to five) years of life were usually, themselves, subjected to excessive corporal punishment during childhood. We do not need successive generations reflecting themselves like mirrors locked face-to-face down an endless corridor of despair. All acts generate reactions. Does the beating really shape the child to long-range behavior goals? Could these goals not have been reached better by psychological (in a calm, reasoning based on facts review) rather than physical controls? The therapeutic approach is that of the clinician M.D.—not to blame—just to try to effect a cure. The cure is the sought-for goal of self-control and emotional equilibrium.

Compliance based on law, regulations, or rules is not the answer to control of human behavior. Self-control, self-discipline, the communistic ideal of the withering away of the state (which has not occurred in China or Russia), where police, army, or jails were no longer to be needed, is a dream which man's basically selfish nature apparently will not yet permit. Man's animal nature and selfish egocentrisms make utopian schemes of society unrealistic to expect.

Perhaps the theory of Doctor B. F. Skinner will in time prevail even in the United States: man will be rewarded (reinforced) for desired behavior and non-rewarded, even punished severely, for deviant behavior. This may be for us a minimum of personal freedom, closed-circuit input for all news, unapproved ideas not to be circulated, man's very existence subject to minute controls, and society regimented as is notably the case in China and elsewhere even today. To be sure, V.D. may be largely eliminated, a minimum of low-quality health services may be available (from so-called barefoot doctors), there will be no unemployment, and slums will largely disappear, but at a cost. The cost is the loss of individual freedom; the collective state absorbs the individual with loss of his identity. Civil rights would vanish.

All actions beget reactions; hurts inflicted on immature juveniles are especially to be avoided for they jeopardize the entire life projections of the youth. Emotional scar tissue from official sanctions (e.g., The First Arrest) prejudice later adjustments and handicap individuals who have no legitimate cause for such lifelong social stigma to be held against them. Juvenile records should be for confidential police use only and expunged at age twenty-one, as most states now require.

The central problem in this discussion of punishment as a social phenomenon is that of the philosophy of life held by both the punisher and the punished (a philosophy of life is a set of values, a frame of reference, a pattern of solutions which are internalized and which guide behavior). If one believes that gung ho bulldozer tactics pay off, then direct physical action will likely be resorted to in problem solving. If more indirect, gentle, and dispassionate behavior has been rewarded by greater success, this pattern will dominate. In police, corrections, or social work there is little doubt that the latter course is to be preferred.

The day when confrontation and adversary-type encounters paid off has long passed. Today's public will no longer tolerate uncouth or aggressive behavior patterns by public servants, and such behavior can only be counterproductive. We need to use the medical model—to cure, not to make more sick. Respect and security are key words to describe optimum interpersonal relations. Corporal punishment of youths and adults has no place in this picture.

We have surely progressed from caveman days and we must hope that man can someday truly be Homo sapiens—the "thinking man" who can reason. This day of enlightened interpersonal relations, of man's humanity to man, will only be achieved when current ideas of the value of punishment are no longer believed and enforced by laws of primitive eras.

Unfortunately, the above views are not held by some judges, police, teachers, corrections, and welfare personnel. So-called hard-nosed views are difficult to change. Perhaps the key idea of this book is this: that "men of good will" in positions of authority and decision making must interact with humanity and compassion in adversarial confrontations such as arrest situations, counseling sessions, and case-work visitations. That there are children with problems, not problem children, has long been wisely observed. Our aim must be to treat the sick behavior, not aggravate the condition. We must proceed from where the respondent (if a minor) or the accused (if of majority age) now is, with all thought of recriminations, stigma, and retribution put entirely out of mind. Judges should consider the cases of convicted persons not only on the basis of what was done but with regard for who the defendant is. This will result in many convicted persons not going to jail at all, who would otherwise be jailed for that offense; at the same time, some persons not incarcerated, or incarcerated for brief periods, would be held much longer, perhaps for decades or life, in confinement because of their chronic psychopathic condition or defective life-style, which has not yet responded to treatment. Only the courts can enforce laws, not the police.

There is a definite groundswell of public opinion in the direction of much less incarceration for long terms where there is reasonable expectation of rehabilitation, and in favor of local handling of antisocial and criminal acts through halfway houses, heavy use of probation, and all-out community efforts to reintegrate offenders into a rehabilitated status. Denmark is a notable example today where long imprisonment has been almost completely abandoned. Rehabilitation means to make able again. Where it is truly a therapy, a refitting of physical and mental powers, "REHAB" has had much success and offers much promise for the future. Some less-than-total results relate to short time spans in therapy, failure to follow up cases, and lack of funds for more intensive efforts where full success may have been achieved, with both physical and mental goals.

The prison is the poorest environment we could devise for treating sick minds and disorganized personalities; prisons are dealing with a clientele (inmates) who have largely already had a lifetime of failure.

The reconditioning of such persons by overworked staffs and in the vicious criminogenic surroundings inevitably indigenous in confinement institutions indeed presents a tremendous challenge and represents an almost impossible task. Recidivism rates of over seventy percent are not surprising, given the task and means to deal with the goal of rehabilitation for the two and one-half million who pass through our prisons each year and of the one million who are continuously confined.

Diversion to rehabilitation centers as an alternative to confinement should be used if feasible. Confinement ought to be the restrictions necessary to isolate the offender, pending adjudication. Electronic leg and "beeper" monitors are used in many places to control mobility.

The issue of capital punishment (execution) is today much in the public's eye. How can society take a life which may be later redeemed and be of even great value? But the fact of deterrence may do some good, for if the hangman's noose dangles before one, it may cause second thoughts for some; for most murderers it is of no deterrence value. Capital punishment has been declared to be a violation of the provisions in the Constitution of the State of California against cruel and unusual punishment. However, some other states which at one time dropped the death penalty have reinstituted it recently.

Abolishment of capital punishment would call for an adequate deterrent system to take its place, a system that would guarantee the protection of the innocent. What such system has yet been proposed or proven?

Today's society is not yet ready to close prisons. Regretfully, confinement appears to be the only interim solution for those who, for a variety of reasons, cannot conform to requirements of the free world. Perhaps, in time, with much better family life, child-rearing practices, schools, job training, and retraining, improved job availability, adult education, substance abuse control, and better public health, the prison will be largely outdated. Hospital custody and care for defectives will always be required for some, but this will be for humane reasons, not punishment.

G. B. Shaw once said: "To punish a man you must injure him; to reform a man you must improve him, and men are not improved by injuries."

Chapter 10

AIDS

In 1993, AIDS became the leading cause of death among Americans 25 to 44 years old, according to the Centers for Disease Control and Prevention. More than 441,000 Americans have been infected with AIDS since 1981 and more than 250,000 have died. In 1993, about 35 of every 100,000 young adults have died of AIDS, with impact greatest in New York, Miami and Atlanta. Young people with AIDS are largely Black and Hispanic, especially those who caught the disease heterosexually.

A lot can be done about it: awareness of heterosexual as well as homosexual transmission routes; that contaminated needles used by addicts must be seen as an AIDS threat; that we must face the dangers of widespread unprotected teenage sex. HIV/AIDS is spreading out of control at about 20,000 new cases every three months. Since the spread is predominately among youths, the impact of AIDS deaths goes far beyond their actual numbers, as Doctor Harold Jaffe of CDC stated.

Fears of limiting the civil liberties of those living with HIV/AIDS have up to now prevented local, state and national public health authorities from identifying infected persons by available results of routine testing daily, in thousands of blood testing stations nationwide, and prevented notifying such persons of their own perilous conditions and informing their sexual and/or needle partners (with strict confidentiality) of the possibility of infection by the HIV/AIDS virus. No invasion of privacy is involved. Each infected case must be identified and each contact followed up in a case study method similar to the way which has been effective in hindering the spread of other sexually transmitted diseases (STD).

All persons tested anywhere and found to be HIV/AIDS positive (some may not be identified then because their cases may be latent and/or of recent infection) should be told of their possible risk. We must not depend on voluntary notification by positives to sexual and/or needle partners.

Partner elicitation is not enough. Public health authorities should, by law, be required to inform all persons at risk of the fact that they may possibly be infected by the virus and to suggest therapy as may be available. Laws to require such notifications are not in effect now (1995). This will be difficult but should be attempted.

There is no reason for any person to avoid responsible behavior. Adults (or of minor ages if mentally competent) can (and should) be charged with murder if they knowingly infect another with AIDS. Some states already have this law. It would apparently apply to cases where infection can be traced to sexual or needle contacts.

Some people have said that we don't have to worry if we're white, heterosexual and adult. But AIDS is a threat everywhere: blood transfusions cannot be guaranteed by your hospital to be free of contamination, and hospitals are running short of blood donations. If you need a blood-volume expander to save your life (accident or ER), or other transfusion therapy, sterile substitutes for whole blood may not be available. No rational solution to end the spread of AIDS seems available. Is society destined to suffer the ravages of this terrible modern plague without help from modern science?

A February 1995 report from the Centers for Disease Control and Prevention states: "More and more women are contracting AIDS through heterosexual sex as the spread of the disease dramatically increases among women in the United States, health officials say."

AIDS cases among women are increasing by about 17 percent a year, and the increase shows no sign of slowing down, the Centers for Disease Control and Prevention has reported. The growth of the disease is leveling off in the population as a whole.

"Women themselves don't have the awareness that they're at risk," said Doctor Diana Dell, an obstetrician-gynecologist who is president of the American Medical Women's Association. In 1994, women accounted for 14,081, or 18 percent, of the 79,674 new AIDS cases among adults. There were 16,798 new cases among women in 1993, but that number was inflated by the expanded definition.

On February 2, 1995, the CDC reported that among all Americans, the AIDS epidemic is stabilizing at a 3 percent annual increase.

Forty-one percent of infected women reported contracting AIDS through intravenous drug use, while 38 percent reported contracting AIDS from a male partner. The number involving a male partner will continue to escalate, Fleming said.

"We have to empower the women to be safe regardless of what their partners are doing," said Dazon Dixon, executive director of Sisterlove, an Atlanta AIDS group for women.

"I tell the women that come in here that there are only two kinds of people in this world: people living with AIDS and people at risk for HIV. Those not already infected can make a choice about which they want to be," she said.

Chapter 11

HANDGUNS

Laws are imperatively needed to forbid anyone other than a peace officer to possess a handgun outside his or her home. Guns are more deadly and more poisonous by far than rattlesnakes or AIDS. The daily tool of children killed by drive-by shootings, school shootings, and gun accidents is a national disgrace not suffered by any other developed or developing country. Children of minor ages must not be permitted access to any guns, especially handguns. Parents and guardians must be held criminally negligent for such access by children under their charge, just as for truancy, arson, assaults and other delinquent acts by their children. All that is needed is a law, strictly enforced, to require that handguns remain in the home, which is the only place they deserve to be, and under strict adult control at all times, day and night.

Chapter 12

SELF-REPORT

The following self-report was written by a young man in prison. A self-report is a method of gathering information about people's behavior, especially illegal behavior, by asking them to report their own past activities; most often it is contrasted to studies of office data such as arrest rates or drug treatment entries (Inciardi, p. 209).

> Take a hit, and come alive
> It's got you hypnotized
> Another one you can't think
> You're going down, you're on the brink
> You close your eyes, you can't see
> It'll hook you, it hooked me
> So buy some crack and take a hit
> And once you start you'll never quit
> Well you may quit and may quit soon
> Feel your heart, Thump, Thump, Boom

I'm starting this report with a poem I wrote about five years ago when in a rehab. It is just saying that once you start it's very hard to quit and if you do, you had better hope it's on your own will. I've known a few who died when their heart exploded while smoking.

From as far as I can tell (remember) it all started way back in '83 when I decided I was going to smoke cigarettes. Why? Because it was—you know—cool. When Johnny Dell introduced himself while smoking a cigarette, I knew he was going to be a friend. I couldn't smoke at home, so I needed a place to smoke in peace (his room). One day he pulled out some weed. Now what did he do that for? That is the first time I smoked weed.

Johnny's dad was an alcoholic and let Kenny drink—even bought beer for us to drink. So now I'm smoking weed and drinking all thanks to Johnny. Pretty quickly it was getting to where I wanted weed and alcohol all the time. When Johnny didn't have any, I chose to steal anything and everything from anywhere. It was partly to have weed and alcohol and partly to show Johnny I'm down with the money thing and to show him it's no problem.

By that time I was hurting my dad mentally and financially. All the while I was going to school (ninth grade), I was smoking, drinking, and stealing. In the process I was introduced to diet pills—speed— that were not expensive (8 for $1), but the caffeine would have me moving a hundred miles an hour. So at age 14, I'm stealing, smoking, drinking—moving at 100-plus miles per hour. Then, I kicked into the second stage that I call "the act."

First let me tell you my background. I was born in the Midwest in 1968. My birth mother was a white teenager; my birth father was a black drummer in a band. I was told that my birth mother tried to keep me. She kept taking me from the adoption agency and then taking me back when things got rough. Apparently, she wanted my father to marry her, but he wouldn't. Anyway, when I was about eight months old, the agency convinced her to sign away her rights to me so that I could be adopted and given a stable home life. My adoptive parents are both white and very well educated; I have an older brother who is also white and very successful at school. I never really fitted in.

Then my adoptive parents got a divorce, so I was shuffled back and forth between their houses—every weekend I would spend with my dad. He remarried when I was about nine years old. Since I was already having trouble in school and in the neighborhood, my parents decided that it would be best for me to live with my dad. That was fine with me—even when he and I then moved to the East Coast it was okay. Then, we moved to a small town where I was the only black person in my school.

I was the bad ass black boy who wanted respect and all. I wore a leather jacket and flashed a switchblade along with my bad mouth. I'm not sure why I chose this act, but keep in mind the drugs and all. Pretty soon I convinced myself that I *was;* instead of acting, I just *was.* The act meant you didn't like school. You can't when you're a bad ass. A bad ass can't like school, does drugs, drinks, smokes, doesn't listen to parents, steals, and does extremely stupid and dangerous stuff to seem cool in his own eyes. If it was good and cool, other people saw it as stupid and couldn't understand. Once into the act, it was impossible to get out. It was all in my head, but I was moving too fast to stop. I needed friends and I got all the wrong ones.

This went on a few years as I failed classes and made my dad more and more angry. He took me to a counselor who was cool, too. We kicked back and talked about how bad life was. In the meantime, my drug use was more and more frequent. I failed the ninth grade, got kicked out of driver's education because I was caught smoking, and was failing ninth grade for the second time when I went to visit my mom who had moved to Texas. While I was down there, my father called and said the school didn't want me back. That meant I was stuck in Texas.

So there I was with no friends. All I had was a drug and alcohol problem. That would have been the best time in my life I think to get help. Unfortunately, no one knew how bad I really was. I mean they knew, but they didn't know. My mom took me to a counselor to try to find out if I was on something. He was easy to con. All I had to do was tell him about being the only black person in a white world and he "knew" what my problems were. Anyway, I didn't get help because I really didn't want it. Instead, I got my GED and looked around for drugs and alcohol.

I got a job at a car wash. The man who ran the car wash knew a man named Pooksie who sells weed. Bingo!

Now Pooksie and I hit it off. I helped him sell a little weed so I could smoke and drink with him. He took me under his wing, and I met almost all the major drug dealers in town. That included *cocaine.* Somebody gave me a joint with 'caine in it and it took me to a new level which was great because the weed and alcohol had become so ordinary. What I call *the hit* is the very first taste I ever had of crack cocaine. It was undoubtedly the best one too. There could only be one more major hit like the first and that's the one that would blow my heart up. But until that major hit, I think I'll always want to get that hit again and again and again. Crack somehow stimulates the brain in a way that's hard to explain, but it leaves me thinking of how to get some more. That became a serious mission. They say that it takes over your pleasure center and eventually you'll only be able to feel pleasure when you hit crack. Whenever some money hit my hand during the past few years, my stomach would start churning and I would cough and gag as I anticipated a hit of crack.

My first hit brought a welcome change to my life. As I said, marijuana and alcohol had become stale, but crack was more expensive, so the old me resurfaced in full effect as robbing and stealing became second nature. "The act" was still present. Since I've never been big, I thought I had to prove my strength in guts. If you ask me, I'm a damn good actor. I kind of had by then convinced myself that I was what I wanted to be. But you see I now realize somewhere in between I had stopped acting. I had become the bad ass black boy who robbed and stole, lied and acted exactly the way I was acting. I'm just now seeing this.

Next, a girl came into my life who was perfectly aware of who I was. Charlene thought that dealing drugs was okay as long as there was money coming to her. She didn't know I used more than I sold. We got an apartment and tried to get along. I guess she tried harder than I did. We stayed together for four and a half years. A lot of it is kind of fuzzy because when I got a job, it was at a gas station with Pooksie fixing tires. I bet for anyone who ever saw Pooksie and me at work it would be hard to believe that from 8 a.m. to 6 p.m. we drank and did drugs (marijuana and cocaine). When I got home, I wanted to get higher. That's what cocaine does for you. Fights ensued and I stole from Charlene and the kids because they were closest.

Then I moved on to manipulating anyone and everyone I could. Oh, Charlene did not mind as long as she got some money out of it. I could do some drugs at home when she had money in her pocket. When the money ran out, our real troubles began. I became extremely violent when confronted about my addiction. I went through a series of major catastrophes. I lost jobs, quit jobs. Charlene started cheating; I started cheating on her. I wrecked a new car because I could not afford insurance. It just went from bad to worse. Skip back a bit.

Charlene had a child and then another one, so the money problem got bigger with child financial responsibilities. I wanted to do right by my kids. I didn't want them to be put in foster homes or adopted. But, I couldn't seem to stop my behaviors. I spent money—lots of money—that we didn't have. That explains why Charlene started getting more upset than usual about drugs: it was cutting into her ability to have money.

As it continued, I guess I just started feeling hopeless and did more drugs to cover my feelings. But my act had all the people I dealt with fooled. They saw a happy-go-lucky dope smoker who just didn't give a damn. After a few bad incidents and one sort of attempted suicide, I went to a rehab. I'm not sure why because I had not made up my mind to quit doing drugs. As far as I can see, I went to keep Charlene and to keep my parents supporting me. Now I'm being as honest as possible. It's hard admitting to all the devious and manipulative things I've done, not to mention the people I've hurt as a direct result of my addiction.

I went to a series of rehabs. On one occasion I walked out of rehab and went straight across the street and bought some beer. That's how much I wanted to quit. Finally I went to Houston to a rehab, partly because I really wanted it and partly for Charlene and my parents. It lasted about two months. I really was trying to stay clean. And it felt pretty good. I had begun to have hopes and dreams again. All this time I had not talked to Charlene. Maybe that's why I stayed clean. I don't know. I do remember someone in a rehab saying that in order to get clean and stay that way, it's best not to have any relations for 8–12 months. That now makes sense to me. At least it seems when I'm alone and not worried about what a girl is doing, I'm much better off. My mind does not get sidetracked.

Anyway, as soon as I talked to her and the kids, something clicked and I wanted out of rehab RIGHT THEN. So I decided (one of the million or so mistakes I've made) to go to a different rehab that I could work out of to earn money for Charlene so she could bring the kids and move back with me.

Unfortunately, the only place I knew where I could work was a labor hall. Now if you have never been unfortunate enough to see one, it's very—how do you say it—sleazy: people on drugs, alcoholics, bums working for drink money and so on. So what goes with that is drug dealers, prostitutes, and many undesirables like that. Day in and day out, I was mingling with them, fighting a lot to keep what money I had, physically and mentally fighting. The pressure was hell, but I had to work to pay rent. Then I snapped and drank a beer, and then another and another. Every day I let myself drink three beers—only three—after work to relax.

Then one night Charlene called and said she had some money and had to move. She asked if she could move to my town to be with me. Of course I said yes. Somewhere back down the line I tried to lie to myself, saying I could handle everything, but I was fooling myself. I was lonely and I had gotten sidetracked with work and my family.

So she came down. We got a little place, and it was okay for a few weeks. Then I snapped somehow. Out of the blue as I was riding the metro home from work (I'd drunk my three beers as usual), I pulled the string to stop the bus at the street where the crack house was and I went to smoking like a choo-choo train. I still don't know why I did it, but when I had spent all of my money, that was one of the worst feelings in the world. It had been three months since I'd smoked crack. Then I blew it.

I sort of remember what happened next. I started on a binge that lasted months. Charlene and my children left and I moved into the labor hall. Now I forgot to tell you I got hurt on the job, so I got paid every day for doing nothing—nothing at all. I would just show up and watch TV. That led to another drug to play with—Vicodin—and it was a *mother*. I became a walking, talking, smoking, drinking, robbing, stealing zombie for a long time. I can see that now.

It happened one day I had some crack and needed a place to smoke safe from the rollers (police) who frequented the area where I stayed. Someone introduced me to a guy named Harvey who was a smoker and a seller. We got along okay. He sold dope out of a house where he and his girlfriend Lacy lived. I guess they saw potential in me the way I was and introduced me to the dope game—not the one I used to play, but the real one with gangs and dealers who you beep on beepers and they bring $400 of dope to be sold at the house. The dealers would then come back three hours later to pick up the money. I saw both Harvey and Lacy mess up on several occasions and smoke some or all the dope and I'd either go robbing or Lacy would go tricking (prostituting) to get enough money to keep from getting beat up. That way of life lasted a long time.

We smoked and sold every day. Every time that I messed up and smoked too much, I'd make up a lie to tell my mom or dad to get some money to keep from getting beat down or killed over $200 worth of dope. Eventually I needed more protection, so I hurt somebody who had a pistol. Then I took the gun to protect me, Harvey, and Lacy from people on the streets. We were known for always having dope or money. In our area of town, if you had something someone else wanted, that person just tried to get it. I had to prove myself. Because I am so small, a gun and an ax handle talked some real strong arguments in my behalf.

Then came the day Harvey hit Lacy with a two-by-four for staying out too late tricking or something. I went off. I ran him out of his own house because I wanted to kill him and probably would have and he knew it. (He was twice my size.) That shows how absolutely crazy I was. Eventually I let him come home, but when he did, I did not sleep on the floor, he did. I slept with Lacy.

Not too many days later she and I broke into a vacant, fully furnished apartment with lights, gas, and water already on. We took our dope business with us. We had people climbing in our window to buy dope and smoke. Occasionally Lacy would leave with a guy for an hour or two. That made me crazy while she was gone, but she always robbed whoever she left with and came home in a hurry. She always said the best thing for a trick is a trick. For the most part, though, she'd lie to me about how she got money. It was always, "Ho, I did not have to do nothing. I beat him before I had to do nothin."

I was in love with her. When we walked together, robbed together, or did anything, we did it as one. We could be up four days in a row and be outside and have a man walk up who wanted some dope and a girl. I'd sell him the dope without him knowing I loved her. She'd go around the corner to do what he wanted and that's when the devil in me popped out. I'd just go around there and take his money and my dope back. Usually the man would resist and I'd hurt him, in some cases pretty bad.

All I could do to keep Lacy from tricking was to show her that I could take what we wanted. We used to think alike all the time after we got to know each other. I guess the reason that I cared for her so much is that we were living in a battle zone and we were two soldiers from the same army. For survival we depended on each other. The only thing was, we did not try to do anything with the money we got except get high and drunk or pay off dope dealers.

Now here's one example of how things turn on you real quick in the Third Ward, or I guess in any dope game:

It was two o'clock in the morning. Lacy and I saw a man who wanted a dime rock. I sold him a piece of soap for $10. He realized it was soap and wanted his money back. Needless to say, I told him he just lost that money. Then she and I walked to the Bootleg House to get a fifth of Thunderbird. When Lacy saw two guys who wanted a dime rock, I told her that if she wanted the money, get them. I was getting the wine. When I walked around the corner, I saw her hiding by a building. As the two guys came around the corner, I knew she had burned them for the $10, but they found her and one guy slammed her up against a wall. At this time I was running up to where they were, saying, "What's up? What's up? Don't touch her again." I guess fortunately for them I had no bullets at that time so I had left the pistol at the apartment. Just then the first guy turned on me and hit me dead in my eye. I dropped my wine in the street. All I saw was Lacy running around the corner with the second guy following her. Meanwhile, homeboy kept beating me in my eye as I lay on the ground. He searched my pockets and got my money and a big master padlock that I used to hit folks with. He hit me with it. After he got all he could from me, he ran around the corner to the phone where Lacy was calling the police. She thought he was going to kill me. He drop kicked her into the booth, broke a bunch of her teeth out of her mouth with the padlock, took her money, and left. Her mouth was bleeding; my eye was swollen shut. But what did we do? We went back to Bootleg and got another bottle of wine. When the police came, they wouldn't let us ride in the squad car with the wine, so we walked two miles to our apartment. We were a drunken mess. For some reason, though, when we woke up that morning sore as hell, we drank a beer and off we went on a mission to get some money from a sucker or a victim or both.

We lived like that until the day I was arrested. To me we were against the world, fighting a losing battle. When she left for a week, I terrorized the neighborhood. Everybody was steering clear of me from what they say. I don't remember really. She was a part of me.

Then came the night she got mad at me and jumped in the car with a dope dealer she owed money to. I knew she was going to pay her bill with her body. Five hours later, I heard her whispering from around the corner saying, "Jamie. Hurry. Let's go." It turns out she waited until he passed out from drinking and took his keys, 9mm pistol, $375 cash, and seventeen $20 rocks which meant we had to get out fast. She gave me the gun and we got a cab for $60 to another town. We got a room and smoked all the dope and drank and drank. By this time in my life, my brain was not the clearest thing around. I was in need of help, but unfortunately I got a job in that new town three days later.

One day not too long after I had started working, Lacy went to the clinic for a rash she had. It turned out it was syphilis. To top that off, she was found to be HIV positive. I'd been with her almost a year and I loved her. She could not have kids, so we never used protection. I figured I probably would get AIDS too, so I used that to manipulate people. I started lying to my parents, saying that I was HIV positive so when they found out that Lacy had it, they would not scream for me to leave her. I'm real ashamed of what I did and to the length I carried this lie. I almost started to believe it, that's how good of a liar I was. I think I started living my lies and got so deep I couldn't get out. Sort of like when I forged a check, I knew I'd get caught eventually so I did three more. A hopeless feeling takes over and nothing matters.

I lost my job after seven months. I quit paying my light bill because Lacy and I wanted to smoke crack. Sometimes I tried to save money for bills, but crack always won the fight. Lacy and I fought every now and then, mostly about my not wanting her to go tricking and staying out all night, but I could not stop her. I really wish I could. There's a long story about her life, so don't judge her too fast. I'm real worried about her right now because she's still out there and I'm here in jail. In a way I'm lucky to be here. I know she's still struggling to survive, to eat, drink, smoke, and sleep. In a lot of ways, I wish she were locked up where she'd be safe. I've gotten used to protecting her and I know she's been relying on me to protect her. I feel real bad, like I let her down.

In ways, Lacy was part of the reason that I did a lot of wrong, but she was also the reason that I didn't do a lot of things I started to do—mainly robbing businesses. I never did that, not once. And mainly the people I robbed or stole from were in the dope game as I was when I got robbed. That happened on several occasions until I got strapped (carried a gun). Living on the street, I guess I became hardened to others' feelings. I just didn't care as long as I got *mine.*

I guess you could say a lot of it had to do with wanting respect, only I wanted respect from all the wrong people. I think once I had done so many things wrong maybe all the way back in the eighties, I lost respect for myself. Once I lost that, it seemed hopeless. I tried to cover how I felt and make my mom and dad think something different was my problem. I don't think I could have lasted much longer the way I was going. I am kind of glad to get out of it except for losing the most important person in my life. Now it may seem like my kids weren't on my mind during this whole deal, but they were. I kept saying when I do this or when I do that I'll send some money or I'll go visit, but that day never came. Every now and then my mind would clear up a bit and I would think about how I'd like to get away and take Lacy with me. I need to have someone else with me for some reason. I might be scared to do it by myself or something. When I think of it all, I cry a lot. Why I don't know exactly. I wonder if I'll ever get over the last 12 years of my life.

What some people might not realize is that when you've lived the way I have, prison does not make me pay for my crimes. Living that way and having to remember is punishment enough, because hell is on earth even with as much as I thought at times I was enjoying life. I was not happy with myself at a very early age. I have a brother who everyone thought was wonderful. I had successful parents. I think deep down somewhere inside I was sure I'd never be as good as my parents wanted me to be, so in order to keep them from having high hopes, I'd mess up things for myself, sabotage my own life. There are a lot of things and reasons for the things I've done. I know that people care for me in many ways, but there is something very important missing. I don't know what it is, but I know it's something that is going to take a while to find. It is eating my insides up. I feel like something is dying in me and I don't want it to.

Right now I'm scared as hell, thinking that I'm going to really have to turn my life around. I've got too much to lose and so much to gain. It's a very scary feeling even with support knowing that I've got to do it alone and I'm not sure how. I think about God sometimes, but that scares me too. I don't know enough about Him not to be scared. It also scares me how self-destructive I get when I'm frustrated and scared. Right now I'm using self-control in jail because I'm not getting the respect I want from some. I'm trying not to care what people think. But young people nowadays in the "game" test each other to see where the other ranks on the respect scale. I'm used to being a 10, or trying to be a 10. Right now I'm a 5. They don't know how far and long to test me. But I know what they don't and sometimes it scares me too!

Sleeping also scares me a lot. I have some very awful dreams. Some nights I have wonderful dreams about people I've loved and had good times with. That also scares me a lot! I've gotten to where I wake myself up most of the time either way. I dream, but I cry or feel like crying. It's so hard to be hard. That's what I've become: hard and cold. It comes and goes. It's like a mode I get into. Once I get started, I go haywire. My parents have seen it in some ways how destructive I can be from an early age. So that makes me sometimes think there's more to my self-destructiveness than drugs and alcohol.

Sometimes I think I'm plain crazy. Now this may sound funny, but I wonder about split personalities. Like when I went crazy and tried to beat the life out of my kids' mother or when I broke the nose of Lacy about a year ago. I've jumped on guys, girls, anyone who happened to be around. As a matter of fact, the day I broke Lacy's nose, I did it in my best friend's house where I was living, and when he tried to stop me, I beat him up as well. Where I get the strength I don't know. It's incredible how I change, and that is probably the scariest aspect of all: not knowing why and how I get so out of control because when out of control, I don't think, love, feel, or care about anything.

I don't know if what I've written will do anyone else any good. I don't know if it has done me any good at this point. It's painful to think about what I've done, what I've become. The respect I was looking for all of my life was a hollow thing, a false thing because the only respect I ever got was based on fear; the only happiness I truly felt was caused by drugs; and in spite of my trying to convince myself otherwise, my first love—my only real love—is alcohol and other drugs. I've thrown away all other chances for real people love. My only hope now is to work to get myself truly clean and stay that way so that maybe some day I can develop a personal relationship that is open, honest, trusting, and good. Pray for me.

Chapter 13

THE JUVENILE OFFENDER:
WHO, WHAT, WHERE, AND WHY IS HE?

1. THE JUVENILE OFFENDER: WHO IS HE?

The juvenile offender is anyone who commits a crime or antisocial act that is still legally a juvenile. Generally this includes people below the age of 15. Recently we've seen youth as young as six years involved with drugs and theft. The age span of the juvenile offender seems to get broader.

* * * * *

He is a person, usually between the ages of six and whatever is considered to be the age of adults (in the state in which one resides), who has either been adjudicated delinquent or found guilty of violations of the law. Perhaps he is merely responsible for behavior which is considered detrimental to the best interests of himself or other members of either his own or the adult society in which he lives. Most of these people are males; however, females are more frequently becoming guilty of types of behavior which may be considered irresponsible.

He moves within a subculture which may have created a milieu of morality in which violations of the establishment norms of behavior have positive connotations—and in which he is encouraged by feedback which reinforces acting-out behavior which is contrary to the long-range best interests of himself and the groups of ideas against which he is reacting. He is a person nearly physically mature who is trying to focus his energies in a manner which actually bears greater resemblance to a child than an adult.

Index offenses are "garden variety" misdemeanors common during adolescence: petty thefts, running away, truancy, staying out late, using alcohol, engaging in sexual conduct, disobeying parents—by persons below the legal age of adulthood, most commonly age 18. These are crimes only for juveniles.

94

He is usually a male offender and engages in an increasing amount of crime each year. He is sometimes, but not as a rule, in a position of wealth or power. He is a young person between the ages of 10 and 18 or 21 who has not been acculturated. He has not learned the basic values of society in an internal sense, and he rebels at the *straight* world. He, most often than not, commits crimes in the company of others like himself. He is of average intelligence and body type, although the Gluecks found a slight predominance of athletic types in their delinquency studies. He is also likely to be a school dropout. If he is black or Mexican-American, near-Eastern or Oriental, he suffers a greater risk of becoming delinquent than if he is white.

Boys are ages 10–17 and girls are ages 12–16, and half are 6–21 years of age who commit status offenses. He may be in counterculture groups such as drug addicts.

He may be a young teen who has been brought up and feels no conscious wrong in what he does. He really doesn't know who he is. His id (i.e. pleasure center) takes over his ego, and most of the time his super ego (that concerned with conscious and social factors) doesn't influence his behavior.

* * * * *

The juvenile offender is technically defined as a male between the ages of 12 and 18, or a female between the ages of 12 and 17, that violates a law, federal or state. But he is more than that. He is a person who may or may not have been caught. I think that probably every person who has ever lived could at some time during his delinquent years be classified as a juvenile offender, for we have all broken a law, social or written, at some time during these years. Here we are concerned with the less fortunate ones: the ones that have been caught, that society is aware of.

The serious offender usually comes from a broken home, cares for no one but himself, will not go to school, may be violent at times, and show signs of hostility, egocentric gratification, or he may be arrogant or rebellious.

2. THE JUVENILE OFFENDER: WHAT IS HE?

The juvenile offender is an antisocial, alienated youth. He rejects the present social norms and adopts attitudes of indifference and aggression. He isn't concerned with the result of his actions and he will be aggressive when necessary to get what he wants. He lives on the spur-of-the-moment impulse. His desires are his motivation for his actions. Reason isn't used. Morals and ethics are something he expects to be treated with, but he doesn't give a thought to a morally wrong action.

He is generally a product of his environment. His parental guidance was so lacking that he has adopted a hedonistic attitude. His life is self-centered. Long-range goals are lacking. His life is so meaningless that this furthers his frustration and he more ardently pursues his hedonistic style.

* * * * *

He is a source of irritation to law enforcement and to the general society. He is a waste to society in many ways: he does not get a complete education, probably will not hold a responsible job, does not willingly enter the armed forces, does not accept the main values of society, and does not seek help for his predicament. He drains money from the economy in the form of all the services rendered for him or to him in the juvenile justice system. He has sometimes become a threat to life and property in public schools, large cities, and occasionally small towns. He has increasingly become a drug user, which will boost his crime potential if he takes expensive drugs. Last but not least, he is likely to become an adult offender if he continues in his accustomed life pattern.

* * * * *

The offender may be, and probably is, sick. This may be either psychological or physical or both. This person may be psychotic, rebellious, and refuses not only to adjust to society but rather wants society to adjust to him.

The juvenile is a problem of society and must be coped with. He can be helped through re-education, rehabilitation and reintegration.

The one thing we must not forget is that juvenile offenders are human beings and with the correct mediation by society they may be turned into useful and productive individuals, and eventually adults. The offender may often be an un-person—uneducated, unclean, unhealthy, unemployed, and unwilling to change. He may not care about anything or anybody but himself. But he can be helped. Retribution to get even with offenders is not ever to be the goal society should seek. Punishment often makes rehabilitation more difficult or impossible to achieve.

Who are the violent juveniles? Studies show that they were likely abused as children, have alcoholic or criminal parents who divorce or separate, live in poor housing, do poorly in school, and lack training and opportunity to work.

* * * * *

◦ He is the child of a society which is also in a great state of flux—more likely than not the product of a set of environmental circumstances which contain greater-than-normal odds of producing an individual whose natural reactions to his environment will be to rebel against the situation he grew up in. He is the cause of much crime which occupies the activities of his local police department. He is the reason for the existence of the entire concept of the juvenile court system—perhaps the bane of his parent's existence—though this is not necessarily so. Some parents would prefer not to learn even of his whereabouts. Many parents are indifferent and hostile to curfews. Many homes have no regular times for meals together or for bedtimes. He may have terrorized his parents and is out of control.

He is a young person whose greatest threat to life is the danger of his own suicide. He may become a resident in the juvenile detention system . . . where he is less likely than elsewhere to gain control of his life. . . . He is the victim of his own powerful emotional drive to find a place for himself, contentment, a way of life, a style of life, a satisfactory sexual adjustment. Lacking the maturity and opportunities an older person might have to cope with the same problems—he becomes the problem.

3. THE JUVENILE OFFENDER: WHERE IS HE?

He is usually located in a broken home. He normally flourishes in large cities where control over his behavior is more difficult. He is more often found in inner-city and ghetto areas and on the street, evading curfew and truant. If apprehended, he can be found in juvenile court, in detention homes, in halfway houses, in reform schools and other facilities provided for him by the state. In general, he is in a big mess. He has lately found his way into the spotlight of public attention.

* * * * *

He may be an inmate in the state department of corrections, the juvenile detention system, the state hospital, the unfortunate occupant of the county jail in the absence of more appropriate detention facilities— and every small town and large city contains people of his age group. He may be found trespassing on government or private property or smoking marijuana in his own bedroom or under a bridge; shoplifting with his friends or planning with a warped mind a lonely suicide or murder. . . . He is frequently found in a car—likely as not, somebody else's. He may be next door or 3,000 miles away in a commune which he hopes will conceal his whereabouts from his parents. He may be in school, or he may not have been for years—though the odds that he will find destructive behavior appealing decreases with the time spent in school. Should he ever become a resident of the State Department of Corrections, he will find most of his companions have not graduated from any school. They are non-readers.

He may be found throughout history. The early Greeks and Romans were also concerned about the behavior of their young people.

He is anywhere along the social ladder—from the poverty-ridden ghetto, or middle class, and even the upper class of society. Mentally, he is where he thinks he can belong. Physically, he's on the street, hanging around pool halls, street corners—anywhere he can be at the moment. Finally he is in a patrol car, then to juvenile court, and into a reformatory. If the process has reached this far, he may be nowhere. He is always where he isn't wanted. The place where he should have been since he was born—in a good home where he can be provided for, cared for, guided correctly, and most importantly, loved—is absent. His teeth and personal hygiene are ignored.

The juvenile offender in the final analysis is the real unperson— unwanted, unloved, underdeveloped, unhealthy, and a misfit in many areas of his own maturation process.

* * * * *

He is found where almost 80 percent of crime is: in the Ghettos. He meets all the *street* people there. Most often he is in metropolitan areas where there is overcrowding, insufficient recreation and unhealthy living places. He is surrounded by dysfunctional people.

Most of the time you find a juvenile who has been *caught* in detention homes, trade schools, or behind bars.

Where there is a sick parent, you find a sick child.

4. THE JUVENILE OFFENDER: WHEN IS HE?

In recent decades the rate of delinquency has greatly risen. You have delinquents when there is overcrowding—when there is little prepared convenient recreation, when people, or his family don't give him the 3 L's: love, limitations, and let them grow up. You have a delinquent when he's been battered for a variety of reasons—a usual one, deficient sphincter control from tender age (less than 3)—or from a parent who transfers his own problems to the child, for severe punishment.

* * * * *

He exists whenever society has not prepared itself to cope with the erratic emotional states of young people—whenever there is a vacuum in the life space that must be immediately filled in the mind of the person who feels a lack. He exists when parents are too busy or too over-protective; when young people must be alone—or when they are together. He is the accomplishment of conscious rearing and total negligence. He becomes dangerous to society when opportunity for destructive behavior coincides with subtle psychological drives and motivations common to all young people—and when proper responses to emotional demands have not been conditioned adequately enough to enable him to find instead a proper outlet for his behavior.

5. THE JUVENILE OFFENDER: WHY IS HE?

He is shaped into delinquency when his life is full of negative factors. A ghetto, delinquent peers, dysfunctional home, poor diet, poor examples, no guidance, no help or love, a poor education, no place to spend his idle time, poor companionship, no parents or caregivers with anything to offer. Then we have a potential juvenile offender who is shaped to be that way.

* * * * *

He may exist simply because his parents or caregivers have not been able to discover an adequate way of meeting their own needs. The unwilling victim of smother love; rejected when he should have been accepted; undisciplined by a father figure; left too much to his own devices by one or both parents; discouraged by what he sees society as consisting of—he seeks to preserve himself by striking out at what he thinks has caused the situation. He may be the unconscious victim of his own drives, never realizing he will destroy himself long before he will ever change anything else.

6. WHAT HAVE BEEN THE OBJECTIVES (AIMS) OF THIS COURSE?

The aims of this course have been to acquaint the student with the environmental and psychological causes of destructive maladjustive behavior in young people. . . . We have probed the larger society of the unpeople of the ghetto, the smaller society of the family, the educational community, and the peer group with a view toward discovering the long-range effects of these institutions as well as discovering ways some of these influences might be altered for the better.

We have discussed the psychological discoveries of Freud, the implications of our unconscious motivation, the efficacy of the approach to behavioral conditioning and have been reminded of the possible physiological problems connected with behavior—brain damage from disease, from substance abuse, and, perhaps, incarceration without therapy.

This course was designed to help us see the child as an omnibus in which all of his life experience and ancestry ride in a perilous journey from birth to death.

* * * * *

We need to re-establish America's personal goals. We need an emphasis on respect, consideration, love and affection. At present we are inner-directed toward monetary values. If we continue in a hedonistic direction we will continue in the juvenile delinquent-crime world we have established. Education is light, ignorance is darkness.

Chapter 14

INSTRUCTOR'S SECTION

INTRODUCTION

An instructor's manual for any textbook should justify its printing and careful consideration by using instructors. The author's experience with the subject matter and familiarity with teaching aids related to the text should qualify him for such a task.

This manual parallels the format of the text in that it avoids wordiness and covers only basic essentials. In no sense is it to be considered as a prescription to be followed without modification by the instructor. It is suggestive, only, based on the author's recent decade of teaching precisely this subject matter to thousands of college-level pre- and in-service students in police, corrections and social rehabilitation courses related to behavioral science.

The author's four decades of experience as a professional educator is condensed herein; hopefully its contents will merit consideration for planning and classroom application. Ideas and insights have been classroom-tested, revised, and found to be practicable and effective with both experienced (in-service) and beginning students of behavioral science.

Each instructor is encouraged to develop and perfect his own teaching methodology. One true axiom for effective teaching is that the more the student does for himself, the more he will learn. A maximum of classroom participation and of discussion is to be encouraged. The usual lecture is the poorest teaching method ever devised. When electricity came into the classroom a revolution in educational methods became possible. A heavy use of multisensory aids to learning is recommended. Particularly where classes meet once a week for a three-hour session, showing one of the suggested films will be found to have great merit; each recommended film has been selected with recency and excellence of content as criteria.

The quiz and examination questions are also furnished solely as suggestions; updating, rearrangement, and adaptation to local conditions is recommended. The nature of this social science subject matter is that it is constantly changing in today's fluid society; instructors are urged to use locally available examples and contemporary cases. A newspaper of national circulation will be an essential reference, for example, *The Christian Science Monitor, The National Observer,* or *The New York Times.*

OBJECTIVES

The text's unique subject matter selection and style of presentation required that only essential behavioral insights be included. It is written for easy assimilation by typical college and police academy students, and a concise yet adequate canvas of the chapter headings has been attempted.

The text is believed to have especial merit for sensitizing new entrants in social service fields to the peculiar social forces operating in the inner city.

The text covers the essential social psychology insights believed necessary for initial safety-minimum role enactment by beginners in social service work as they interface with youth whether in adversary or helping encounters. In-service officers will profit from its insights to the nature, motivating and criminogenic factors operating in today's youths. The main emphasis is that retribution has no role or purpose in relation to juveniles.

The objective of the text is to provide a readable, terse, yet scientifically sound presentation of the who, what, when, where and how of the behavior of today's youthful offender.

METHODS

Perhaps the most criticized aspect of professional education is its emphasis on methodology. The author believes method of instruction is important; learning efficiency can be improved by psychologically sound teaching methods.

The first essential is for the student to be active and individually committed to the learning task at hand. All learning is self-learning. The best instructor can only contrive learning experiences which the learner must work with and react to. Specifically for this course, the essential requirement is for the student to read as widely and intensively as possible the excellent books, periodicals, and newspapers easily available today in college and public libraries and which provide an embarrassment of riches for parallel reading.

Students will find that writing critical evaluations and additions to chapters, based both on their parallel readings and on their personal experiences, will be a challenging and rewarding exercise. The text has been written, in part, by exactly this procedure.

The films listed have been selected for individual excellence. New films are constantly being produced; the task of remaining *au courant* with film output will require the instructor to keep his name on mailing lists from producers and distributors (university film libraries and state film repositories) and from the U.S. Government's National Audio-Visual Center, National Archives and Records Service, Washington, D.C. 20409. Extensive use of films is recommended. We are living in an age when most students have been conditioned to learn easily from films, and many recent and excellent films are becoming available in social psychology.

A final word relative to methodology: the author believes that effective classroom learning largely depends on the fullest participation and expression of ideas by students; "talking at" students is poor pedagogy. The more the students are active, the more they will learn and retain. The text should not be the sole source of ideas; it is designed as a point of departure for amplification—its brevity compels such use.

SAMPLE QUIZ

DEFINE BRIEFLY THE FOLLOWING TERMS:

1. "Smother love" —

2. Alienation —

3. Generation gap —

4. The key ideas of Dr. Freud (List 5) —

5. Glueck's delinquency predictor factors (List 5) —

6. Retributive vs. therapeutic goals —

7. Physiological age —

8. Role theory —

9. Acting-out behavior (with example) —

10. Functional mental illness —

11. Cybernetics —

12. Psyche and soma (define each and tell how related) —

13. Psychosomatic illness—

14. Unconscious psychodynamic motivation (with example)—

15. Organicity—

16. Stress—

17. Mental age (M.A.)—What is its value in school use?

18. Psychopathology—

19. "Programmed" life-style—

20. Pathogenic or criminogenic family setting—

21. Personality—

22. List 10 typical characteristics of adolescents—

    1.   6.

    2.   7.

    3.   8.

    4.   9.

    5.   10.

23. What are the "Three L's?"

24. What is "Condition Red?"

25. Explain substance abuse in terms of 1995 actuality.

SAMPLE FINAL EXAM

FORM B
DIRECTIONS: Answer briefly, adequately, in space provided.
1. List twenty (20) typical characteristics of today's adolescent:

2. How have juvenile courts failed to achieve their hoped-for goals? Why?

3. Discuss psychological explanations relative to sexual deviancy.

4. What are the apparent consequences for both adolescents and society from drug, alcohol and tobacco abuse (including marijuana)?

5. What is today's humanistic attitude toward traditional "punishment" as correction for juvenile criminal acts?

6. How may the serious antisocial effects of negative peer group power be minimized?

7. How may the ghetto's criminogenic environment be aborted?

8. The "school" as a social institution is in trouble. Explain.

9. What are the central ideas of Freudian theory as related to adolescents?

10. How must today's family as a social institution be improved?

REFERENCES

Allport, G.W. (1960). *Personality and Social Encounter.* Boston: Beacon Press.

Bartol, C.R. (1991). *Criminal Behavior.* Englewood Cliffs, NJ: Prentice-Hall.

Belenko, S.R. (1993). *Crack and the Evolution of Anti-Drug Policy.* Westport, CT: Greenwood Press.

Byrum, O. (1992). *Old Problems in New Times.* Chicago, IL: Planners Press.

Carney, F.L. (1989). *Criminality and its Treatment.* Malabar, FL: Robert E. Krieger Publishing Co.

Champion, D.J. (1992). *The Juvenile Justice System: Delinquency, Processing, and the Law.* New York: MacMillan Publishing Co.

Cohn, A. and R. Udolf. (1979). *The Criminal Justice System and its Psychology.* New York: Van Nostrand Reinhold.

Covey, H.C., Menard, S., and Franzese, R.J. (1992). *Juvenile Gangs.* Springfield, IL: Charles C Thomas.

Drug Policy Foundation. (1994).

Ellison, K.W., and Buckhout, R. (1981). *Psychology and Criminal Justice.* New York: Harper and Row.

Freud, S. (undated). *Abstracts of the Standard Edition of the Complete Works of Sigmund Freud.* U.S. Department of Health, Education, and Welfare.

Gay, Peter. (1988). *Freud.* NY: W. W. Norton.

Glueck, Sheldon and Eleanor. (1960). *Predicting Delinquency and Crime.* Cambridge, Harvard University Press.

Goldstein, A.P. (1990). *Delinquents on Delinquency.* Champaign, IL: Research Press.

Grof, G.N. (1994). *The Mad Among Us.* New York: MacMillan Publishing Co.

Inciardi, J.A. (1984). *Criminal Justice* (2nd ed.). New York: Harcourt, Brace, Jovanovich Publisher.

Inciardi, J.A., Howowitz, R., and A.E. Pottieger. (1993). *Street Kids, Street Drugs, Street Crime.* Belmont, CA: Wadsworth Publishing Co.

Institute of Medicine. (1994). *Aids and Behavior.* Washington, DC: National Academy Press.

Kinsey, A.C., Pomeroy, W.B., and Martin, C.E.: *Sexual Behavior in the Human Male.* Philadelphia: Saunders, 1948; and Kinsey, A.C., Pomeroy, W.B., and Martin, C.E.: *Sexual Behavior in the Human Female.* Philadelphia: Saunders, 1953. Masters, Johnson and Kolodny: *Heterosexuality* is a sequel, 1994. New York, Harper Collins, Publishers.

Lazear, D. (1991). *Seven Ways of Knowing: Teaching for Multiple Intelligences* (2nd ed.). Palatine, IL: Skylight Publishing.

Kisker, G.A. (1973). *The Disorganized Personality.* New York: McGraw Hill.

Krisberg, B., and J.F. Austin. (1993). *Reinventing Juvenile Justice.* Newberry Park, CA: Sage Publications.

Lindsey, D. (1994). *The Welfare of Children.* New York: Oxford University Press.

McCaghy, C.H., and Cernkovich, S.A. (1987). *Crime in American Society* (2nd ed.). New York: MacMillan Publishing Co.

Menninger, K. (1963). *The Vital Balance.* New York: Viking Press.

Montemayor, R., Adams, G.R., and Gullotta, T.P. (1994). *Personal Relationships During Adolescence.* Thousand Oaks, CA: Sage Publications.

Nastasi, B.K., and DeZolt, D.M. (1994). *School Interventions for Children of Alcoholics.* New York: The Guilford Press.

National Clearing House for Alcohol and Drug Information. P.O. Box 2345, Rockville, MD 20852. Includes a toll-free, 24-hour hotline to find out where and how to get help for cocaine abuse: 1-800-COCAINE.

National Crime Prevention Council. (1992). *Talking With Youth About Prevention.* Bureau of Justice Assistance, 1700 K. Street NW, Washington, DC 20006.

National Criminal Justice Reference Service, Box 6000, Rockville, MD 20850. Toll-free number: 1-800-851-3420 or 1-800-732-3277 (statistics).

Ranger, T., and Slack, Paul. (1992). *Epidemics and Ideas.* Cambridge University Press.

Reed, W.G. (1993). *Health and Medical Care of African Americans.* Westport, CN: Auburn House.

Rubin, L.B. (1994). *Families on the Fault Line.* New York: Harper Collins Publishers.

Skinner, B.F. (1972). *Beyond Freedom and Dignity.* New York: NY: Knopf.

Sahakian, W.S. (1968). *Psychology of Personality.* Itasca, IL: F.W. Peacock.

Rosenthal, D. (1973). National Institute of Mental Health, Laboratory of Psychology, Bethesda, MD.

Sanberg, D.N. (1989). *The Child Abuse-Delinquency Connection.* Lexington, MA: Lexington Books/D.C. Heath & Co.

Sarason, S.B. (1994). *Psychoanalysis, General Custer and the Verdicts of History.* San Francisco: Josey-Bass Publishers.

Straus, M.B. (1994). *Violence in the Lives of Adolescents.* New York: W.W. Norton & Co.

Trebach, A.S., and Inciardi, J.A. (1993). *Legalize It?* Washington, DC: The American University Press.

Thrasher, Frederick M. (1968). "The Gang." In Richard R. Korn, *Juvenile Delinquency.* New York, Thomas Y. Crowell Co., 1968, p. 6.

Vallance, T.R. (1993). *Prohibition's Second Failure.* Westport, CN: Praeger.

Vold, G.B., and Bernard, T.J. (1986). *Theoretical Criminology* (3rd ed.). New York: Oxford University Press.

Wright, K.N., and Wright, K.E. (1994). *Family Life, Delinquency and Crime: A Policymaker's Guide—Research Summary.* Washington, DC: U.S. Department of Justice, Office of Juvenile Justice and Delinquency Prevention.

U.S. Office of Education, 1917, Wash. DC. *Seven Cardinal Principles of Secondary Education.*

AUDIOVISUAL TEACHING AIDS

Addictive Personality: Who Uses Drugs and Why? (1989). (26 minutes; videocassette), HRC.*

Aids: What Everyone Needs to Know, 2nd Rev. (1990). (18 minutes; videocassette), Churchill Films.*

Alcohol, Drugs and Kids. (1989). (18 minutes; videocassette), Aimes Films.*

Aquamarine to Diamonds, Las Palmas School for Girls, Henry F. Greenberg Productions, Los Angeles, CA. Available from Hollywood Film Company, 956 Seward St., Hollywood, CA 90038.

Before It's Too Late: Teenage Suicide. (no date). (20 minutes; film and videocassette), Walt Disney Productions.

Brain Compatible Learning. (1994). (60 minutes), VJE.*

Business, Behaviorism, and the Bottom Line: A Conversation with B.F. Skinner and *Token Economy: Behaviorism Applied.* Psychology Today Films, CRM Educational Films, Del Mar, CA 92014.

Child Abuse and Neglect: The Hidden Hurt. (1985). (45 minutes; videocassette), Guidance Associates.*

Child of Rage: Story of Abuse. (1991). (30 minutes; videocassette), Home Box Office.

Crack. (1987). (25 minutes, 16mm film), Bailey-Film Associates.*

Crackdown II. (1988). (50 minutes; videocassette), Great Plains National TV.*

Discipline with Dignity. (1991). (20 minutes; videocassette), NEP.*

Drugs & Youth: The Challenge. (1991). (23 minutes; videocassette), available in Spanish and English. CCP.*

Effective Schools for Children At Risk. (1994). (25 minutes; video and training materials). Association for Supervision and Curriculum Development (ASCD).

Effective Schools: Sustaining the Effective School. (1991). (70 minutes; videocassette), EFF.*

Families for Prevention. (1991). (10 minutes; videocassette), EE.*

Gangs, Guns, Graffiti. (1989). (30 minutes; videocassette), PEP.*

Gateways to the Mind, Bell Telephone Company.

Journey in Time, NBC Documentary, 1970 (drug culture, glue, heroin).

Last Chance Ranch, Florida State Department of Corrections, Tallahassee, FL.

Mind of Man, Indiana University Audio-Visual Center, Bloomington, IN 47401.

Miracle of the Mind, McGraw-Hill Films, Manchester Road, Manchester, MO 63011.

---

*Film distributor's name and address may be obtained by contacting Educational Service Center, Region VI, Media Department, 3332 Montgomery Road, Huntsville, TX 77340.

Psychology Today Films: (1) Personality, (2) Abnormal Behavior, CRM Productions, 9263 Third Street, Beverly Hills, CA 90210 (Rental).

Scared Straight. 1979 and 1987 Academy Award winning film.

Suicide: A Teenage Dilemma. (1989). (33 minutes; videocassette), HRC.*

What Can We Do About Violence? Bill Moyers TV Specials January 9 and 11, 1995. WNET.

You've Got to be Kid-Ding: A Look at Adolescents. (1984). (training guide and 8 videocassettes), ATC.*

INDEX